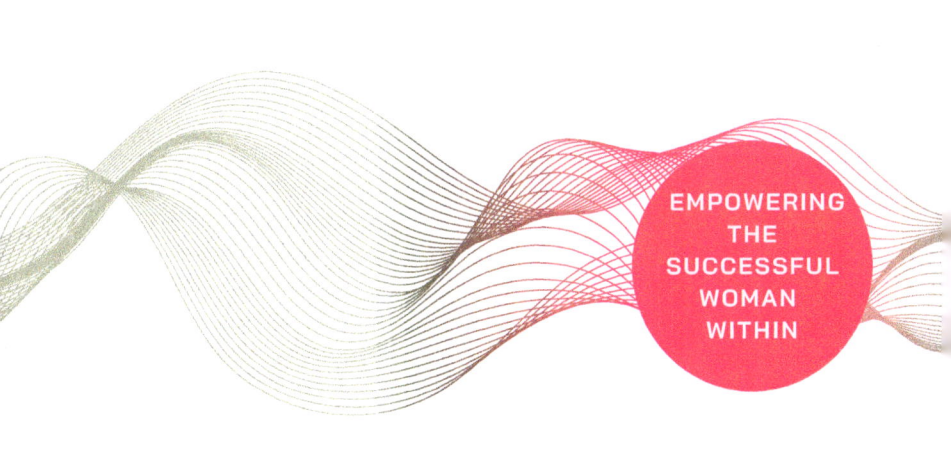

The Ultimate Burn Book for the Successful Woman Within

Written by Tori G Doyle

Copyright © 2024 by Tori G Doyle

All rights reserved. No part of this book may be reproduced in any manner whatsoever without written permission of the publisher.

First Printing, 2024

Published by Tori G Doyle

ISBN 978-0-6486278-3-8

A catalogue record for this book is available from the National Library of Australia

THE ULTIMATE
Burn Book

FOR THE SUCCESSFUL WOMAN WITHIN

WRITTEN BY TORI G. DOYLE

To the incredible women who gracefully carry the weight of the world on their shoulders: Your resilience, compassion, and unwavering commitment do not go unnoticed. You are the epitome of strength and grace. Keep shining your light and know that you are appreciated beyond measure.

About The Book

This book is your go-to guide for juggling it all while keeping your sanity intact. It's all about building a powerful mindset that helps you grow, bounce back, and really get to know yourself—while tackling perfectionism, self-criticism, and that pesky fear of failure.

Mindfully: Tackling Those Mindset Roadblocks
First up, we dive into the mindset barriers that can trip you up. Think of it as your personal GPS for navigating through the mental challenges. Understanding these hurdles is key to leveling up your life.

Spiritually: Tapping into Your Inner Guru
Next, we'll help you connect with your inner self to unleash that growth potential. This section features self-reflection exercises like burning negative thoughts, a 7-day progress over perfection challenge, and journaling and drawing prompts to create distance from negative energy. All these practices will prepare you to clarify what you truly want to manifest.

Purposefully: Manifesting Like a Boss
Now we're getting strategic about manifestation. It's time to set clear intentions and move past self-criticism! With a bit of flexibility and the Momentum Matrix—a framework that helps you put your professional and personal goals into action—you'll be on your way to creating a life that truly aligns with your aspirations.

Together, these sections serve as both a guide and a workbook, allowing you to revisit and reflect at any stage of your journey. Each time you open it, you'll discover something valuable—like a trusty friend cheering you on. So, take a deep breath, embrace your potential, and let this book inspire you to step boldly into the life you envision. Your adventure starts now!

Table of Contents

About The Book ... 05

How to get the most out of your burn book ... 09

Introduction ... 11

PART ONE
MINDFULLLY

Internal Dialogue ... 14

Perfectionism ... 22

Fear of Failure ... 28

Self-Criticism ... 35

Questions ... 41

PART TWO
SPIRITUALLY

Visualisation ... 52

Visualisation In Session ... 61

Manifesting ... 65

Grace and Gratitude ... 70

I Am: Personal Manifesting Mantra ... 76

Celebrating Wins ... 80

The Freedom of "Good Enough" ... 83

Step over Fear ... 94

Journal & Draw Out Your Truth ... 102

Table of Contents

PART THREE
PURPOSEFULLY

Momentum Matrix   130

How To Use The Momentum Matix   141

Case Studies   147

Momentum Matrix Worksheet   169

Gratitude is the Force that Lifts You   181

You Are The Inspiration   188

References   189

Acknowledgement   191

About The Author   192

The Books   193

Connect   194

Flames To Freedom Guided Meditation   196

"Think like a queen.
A queen is not afraid to fail.
Failure is another
steppingstone to greatness."
— Oprah Winfrey

How to get the most out of your burn book

without setting in on fire

How to Use This Book:

Set the Scene

Find a quiet, comfortable space where you can focus and feel relaxed. This is your time to explore, so make it fit for the Queen you are!

Dive into the "What" and "Why"

Begin each section by reading the provided information. This will help you understand the concepts and significance behind your experiences. Take notes or highlight key points that resonate with you.

Reflect Deeply

After each informational section, take a moment to reflect. Use the guided questions to explore your thoughts and feelings. Write down your responses in the space provided. Remember, this is a judgment-free zone!

Transform Your Perspective

As you identify those 'oops' moments, challenge yourself to flip the narrative. What lessons can you extract? How can these experiences serve as steppingstones? Document these insights.

Implement Lasting Strategies

Move on to the strategies section, where you'll find practical exercises designed to nurture your growth. Choose a few that resonate with you and make a commitment to incorporate them into your daily life.

Celebrate Progress

Regularly revisit your reflections and acknowledge your growth. Celebrate your wins, no matter how small. This will reinforce positive change and keep your motivation alive.

Affirm and Inspire

Throughout your journey, make room for uplifting affirmations. You will have your own personal Mantra or use the ones provided. Repeat them daily to shift your mindset and silence that inner critic.

Let's kick off this adventure—your future self will be grateful!

Embrace the process and let each section guide you toward growth and self-acceptance.
Remember, this is not just a book; it's a journey to becoming the best version of you!

Introduction

Hey there, gorgeous!

As you begin this transformative journey through the pages of this book, know that you are not alone. This journey is not merely about overcoming perfectionism, fear of failure, or self-criticism; it's about embracing your authentic self. By honouring your unique journey and choosing self-compassion over harsh judgement, you cultivate self-love and acceptance.

In moments of doubt and struggle, remember that each challenge presents an opportunity for growth. This book will guide you in recognising those moments as invitations to deepen your connection with yourself. When you show up authentically, you create a safe space for your own healing and resilience. Your journey is a testament to the beauty that lies within.

As you navigate this path, may you always remember the incredible impact you possess on your own life. Your grace is a gift to yourself, and your gratitude enriches your soul. Let us embark on this journey to transform our lives and create a world where love and understanding flourish within us. Thank you for being the remarkable woman you are, and for taking this courageous step forward.

–PART ONE–

MINDFULLY

"The mind is everything.
What you think
you become."
					-Buddha

MINDFULLY

Internal Dialogue

The Infamous Internal Trio

Perfectionism Trap

Perfectionism might seem like a noble pursuit, but it can quickly become a hindrance. Spending hours going over marketing plans, lining up the right time to launch a new product, researching 20 options and all the pros and cons for the perfect holiday with the fam, or tweaking a PowerPoint slide that no one will notice is like trying to sculpt the Mona Lisa out of mashed potatoes—exhausting and ultimately impractical.

This relentless chase for flawlessness can lead to burnout faster than you can say "I'm a perfectionist," leaving little room for creativity or risk-taking.

Fear of Failure

The fear of failure often resembles a glaring neon sign that screams, "DON'T EVEN TRY." It manifests as a nagging internal voice that transforms every project into a potential disaster film, with you cast as the director of this cinematic flop. When combined with self-criticism, your wrap party becomes a solo affair, where the only guest is self-doubt and the only thing being served is your insecurities.

Your Inner Critic

Women often face these challenges head-on, trying to quiet the noisiest of these internal challenges, but when one quiets down another will always scream louder. Becoming aware of your internal barriers is the first step in writing a new story where you have full artistic control. After all, success is built on life's experiences, forever evolving. Embrace the journey by focusing on growth rather than perfection. Remember, every misstep is a steppingstone to success. It's time to silence that inner critic and take charge of your narrative.

Let's dive a little deeper

When it comes to pursuing your success, perfectionism, fear of failure, and that persistent inner critic can be huge barriers. These internal challenges can often feel like they're holding back your creativity, confidence, and progress. Understanding their impact and origins is crucial for overcoming them.

Perfectionism might start with societal expectations, where you feel pressured to meet exceptionally high standards in both your personal and professional worlds. Research shows that women often experience perfectionism more intensely due to these societal pressures. This can lead to over-analysis, procrastination, and burnout, which stifles innovation and delays decision-making. Try embracing a mindset that values progress over perfection to free up time and energy for more meaningful pursuits.

The fear of failure is another major barrier, often ingrained from an early age. Studies suggest that girls are frequently socialised to avoid failure more than boys, which might lead to a heightened fear of taking risks.

This fear can result in missed opportunities and a reluctance to step outside your comfort zone. Re-framing failure as a valuable learning opportunity rather than a catastrophe can unlock new paths to success.

Then there's the inner critic, that persistent and often harsh internal voice that can undermine your confidence and contribute to impostor syndrome. This self-doubt might be more pronounced as you juggle multiple roles and societal expectations. By acknowledging this voice and countering it with positive affirmations, you can shift the narrative from self-doubt to self-assurance.

Your brain plays a crucial role in holding onto experiences that shape and reinforce these barriers. Neuroplasticity, the brain's ability to reorganise itself by forming new connections, means that repeated thoughts and behaviours can become deeply in grained. Negative experiences or critical feedback can strengthen neural pathways associated with perfectionism, fear of failure, and self-criticism, making these barriers more persistent.

Societal conditioning further amplifies these effects. From a young age, you might have been taught to prioritise harmony and avoid confrontation, manifesting as internal pressure to conform and please.

This societal backdrop can reinforce perfectionism, fear of failure, and the inner critic, making it challenging to break free and pursue your goals. Chronic perfectionism and fear of failure are also linked to mental health issues like anxiety and depression, creating a difficult cycle to escape. By focusing on growth rather than flawlessness, you can foster resilience and a healthier mindset, paving the way for success on your own terms.

Ultimately, recognising and addressing these barriers is essential for achieving your version of success. By silencing the inner critic, re-framing failure, and letting go of perfectionism, you can take charge of your narrative and craft a path that is not only successful but also fulfilling and true to yourself.

Embrace the Chaos

The Infamous Internal Trio

Navigating life as a woman juggling multiple responsibilities feels like living with a hyper-critical roommate who high lights every flaw. This internal dialogue can be overwhelming, but it's time to silence that negativity!

Embracing the chaos and quieting your inner critic is essential for success—after all, who needs a roommate that constantly critiques your every move?

Alright, let's kick off with some self-reflection!

Think about a recent situation that went completely off the rails.

How did you handle it?

Did you stew over it for ages, or was it more of a "meh, whatever" moment?

What challenges popped up? Did you come in full force like a wrecking ball or did you tippy-toe around these challenges?

Give yourself a break—acknowledge your feelings without playing the blame game.

What did you learn from this little mishap?

How has it changed your outlook or actions going forward?

Maybe you kept your cool when chaos reigned, or you came up with a genius workaround. Celebrating these wins boosts your resilience and self-confidence, because let's face it, we all need a little cheerleading sometimes.

Finally, think about how you can use this newfound insight next time. Set some tiny, doable goals for handling similar situations. Maybe you take a deep breath before responding, call up a friend for advice, or just give yourself a moment to process. Every little step helps you grow and navigate life's ups and downs.

Remember, self-reflection is a journey, not a race. The more you look inward, the better you'll adapt and thrive when life throws you the unexpected.

Perfectionism

"The key to happiness
is letting go of the
idea of perfection."
-Debra Messing

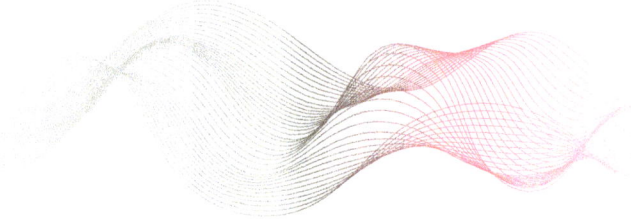

MINDFULLY

Perfectionism

The Double Edged Sword

Perfectionism can be a double-edged sword. As women who do it all, we often set the bar high, expecting ourselves and our teams to deliver nothing short of brilliance.
But, let's be honest, the pursuit of perfection can be a relentless chase, leaving us feeling perpetually unsatisfied and stressed.

While perfectionism can fuel our ambition, it can also stifle our growth. It's the high standards that propel us forward, driving us to sharpen our skills and reach our goals. But the obsession with flawlessness? That's where we stumble. The fear of failing can paralyse us, leading to procrastination or avoiding tasks altogether. Instead of celebrating our wins, we find ourselves fixating on our shortcomings, cultivating a mindset of self-criticism and anxiety. So, how do we strike an agreement?
How do we harness the positive aspects of perfectionism without letting it consume us?

The key lies in progress and development over unattainable perfection. It nudges us to be kinder to ourselves, to see our imperfections not as weaknesses, but as opportunities for growth and learning.
By celebrating the small victories and extracting lessons from the setbacks, we can cultivate a healthier mindset.
One that values our well-being over unrealistic standards.
One that sees the beauty in the journey, not just the destination.
Because being a successful woman isn't about being flawless; it's about being fearlessly authentic.

As we navigate the woman's journey landscape, let's remember that we are not alone.
We are part of an inspiring community of women who are redefining success.
And together, we can turn our ambition into a driving force that fuels not just our passions, careers, and businesses, but our personal growth too. Because the only true perfection is in embracing our imperfections and turning them into our strengths.

Proceed with Caution
comes with side effects

When you strive for perfection, it can sometimes come off as a bit intense, leading people to label you as "A-holes".
Imagine meticulously checking every detail of a project while her team is just trying to survive the Monday morning coffee rush. This relentless pursuit of excellence can create a tense atmosphere where creativity takes a backseat, and everyone feels the pressure to meet impossibly high standards.

On the flip side, this perfectionist streak can also lead to isolation. When a woman is seen as overly critical or demanding, she might inadvertently alienate her team and the people around her leaving her without the support she needs.
It's like being the chef who insists on perfect soufflés while everyone else is just trying to whip up a decent scrambled egg. Instead of building camaraderie, she ends up with a bunch of people who are more focused on avoiding her than on collaboration.
So, while striving for the ultimate result is admirable, there's a fine line between being a driven leader and turning into your version of a fire-breathing dragon.

There is a Sweet Spot

Let's chat about finding the right synchrony between high standards and teamwork, whether it's in your professional or personal life.

It's essential to appreciate the hard work of those around us and foster a culture of open communication.
When everyone feels valued, it creates a positive atmosphere where everyone is motivated to contribute their best.
Think of it as building a supportive network that helps all of us shine, this WILL reflect back into being our best selves.

When you can combine your pursuit of excellence with a bit of empathy, you will often see everyone around you becoming more innovative and productive. Setting clear expectations while also allowing for creativity and flexibility can lead to amazing results. It's all about finding that sweet spot where high standards meet a collaborative spirit.

Ultimately, striving for perfection shouldn't come at the expense of strong relationships. Building a culture of mutual respect can lead to a more harmonious life.

After all, success is much more rewarding when it's shared with others who appreciate the journey together.

what will it cost you?

The pursuit will wear you out and those around you.

Key impacts on your Professional Life:

Increased Stress and Burnout
- The constant drive for perfection can lead to chronic stress, overwhelming feelings, and eventual burnout, reducing overall job performance.

Impaired Decision-Making
- Perfectionists may struggle to make decisions due to fear of making mistakes, leading to missed opportunities or delayed projects.

Career Advancement
- Women may hold back from seeking promotions or new roles due to fear of not meeting high standards, limiting their career growth.

Relationship Strain
- Perfectionism can affect teamwork and collaboration, as perfectionists might have difficulty delegating tasks or accepting others' work.

Imposter Syndrome
- Many perfectionists feel like frauds, leading to decreased confidence and reluctance to showcase their achievements.

what will it cost you?

The pursuit will wear you out and those around you.

Key impacts on your Personal Life:

Impact on Relationships
- High standards can lead to dissatisfaction with partners, friends, and family, causing conflicts and isolation.

Self-Criticism
- Perfectionists often engage in negative self-talk, which can lead to anxiety and depression, affecting overall well-being.

Fear of Failure
- This fear can prevent women from trying new things or taking risks in their personal lives, stifling growth and enjoyment.

Time Management Issues
- Spending excessive time on tasks to achieve perfection can limit personal time and lead to missed social opportunities.

Neglecting Self-Care
- The focus on perfection may lead to neglecting physical and mental health, as personal care takes a backseat to achieving goals.

Fear of Failure

"Failure is not the opposite of success,
it's part of success."
— Arianna Huffington

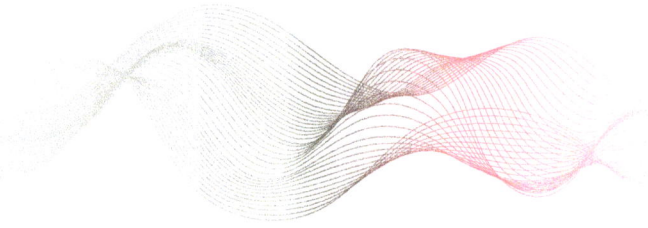

MINDFULLY

Fear Of Failure

The Stepping Stones To Success

Fear of failure is a common gremlin that sneaks into our minds, whispering doubts like, "What if you mess up?" It's a universal experience, often fueled by societal pressures and expectations. Yet, failure is a natural part of our journey, a quirky travel companion that, although annoying, helps us grow and learn. But what if we just didn't grow if we saw failure as just that, a failure? Embracing a growth mindset can transform challenges into opportunities.

One effective strategy against this fear is surrounding ourselves with mentors and peers who openly share their stories of success and failure. These narratives act as a motivational playlist, reminding us that we're not alone on this wild ride. Hearing how others have navigated setbacks can inspire us to persevere and see failure as a stepping stone rather than a dead end.

Celebrating small wins is another game-changer. Instead of fixating on potential failures, focus on the joy of progress. Those little victories, those small fist pumps, eventually lead to significant successes. By acknowledging and appreciating these moments, we build confidence and momentum, making the journey more rewarding and less daunting.

Internally, conquering the fear of failure involves cultivating self-compassion and resilience. It's about giving yourself a mental high-five, encouraging a mindset that sees setbacks as learning opportunities.

Externally, advocating for environments where risk-taking is celebrated rather than shunned can create a supportive atmosphere that fosters growth and innovation.

Representation matters immensely. Seeing women who manage to "do it all" serves as powerful inspiration, proving that setbacks are merely detours on the path to success. Their achievements demonstrate that it's possible to balance career, business, and life, motivating us to pursue our dreams with tenacity and confidence.

Educational workshops and supportive organisations play a vital role in this journey. They provide the tools and policies needed to face uncertainty with confidence, encouraging innovation and risk-taking. These unsung heroes make it easier for women to unleash their full potential, helping us push past fear and continue growing into the incredible forces we are meant to be. So, when fear of failure comes knocking, remember it's just a stepping stone on your path to greatness.

Proceed with Caution
comes with side effects

Fear of failure can feel like that annoying guest at a party who just won't take the hint and leave. It's tough when you're gearing up for a big presentation and that little voice in your head starts chiming in with, "What if they laugh? What if I trip over my own words? What if I accidentally set the office on fire?" It's no wonder you might hesitate to seize opportunities. That fear can really hold you back, making you doubt your talents and capabilities.

And let's talk about the whole "playing it safe" thing. It's so easy to stick to what you know, right? But think about it: choosing to eat plain toast instead of exploring all those delicious toppings is like avoiding risks in your career.

Sure, toast is reliable, but where's the fun in that? By staying in your comfort zone, you might miss out on incredible growth experiences and chances to shine. You have so much potential, and the world needs to see it!

Now, I know it can be tough not to compare yourself to others. When you're feeling that fear of failure, it's easy to look around and see everyone else who seems to have it all together. That can lead to a nasty case of imposter syndrome, making you feel like you don't belong or aren't good enough—when you absolutely are! Instead of letting that fear create competition or feelings of isolation, let's lift each other up. Embrace the wild ride of professional life, because remember: failure is just another word for "learning experience." So, how about we toast to that? (Avocado toast, anyone?)

There is a Sweet Spot

This tricky little thing called fear of failure is like a wild roller coaster ride—exciting but a bit nerve-wracking, right? On one hand, it can stop you in your tracks; on the other, it can actually be a pretty useful motivator. Finding the sweet spot on fear of failure is all about embracing it without letting it hijack your dreams. Just like with roller coasters, a little fear adds to the thrill, but too much? You might end up too scared to get on!

When you learn to harness that fear, it can actually push you to take sensible risks. Instead of avoiding challenges, you start to see them as opportunities for growth. It's like deciding to try that daring new dish at your favorite restaurant instead of sticking with the same old pasta. Sure, it's a risk, but what if it's the best decision ever? By taking those calculated leaps, you can discover new strengths and maybe even surprise yourself with what you're capable of.

And here's the fun part: when you begin to view failure not as a disaster, but as a steppingstone, you'll find your confidence soaring. Each little stumble becomes part of your adventure, and before you know it, you're cheering yourself on. "And she goes for it! Oh, a minor setback, but look at her bounce back!" So, let's embrace that sweet spot where fear of failure meets opportunity. After all, life's too short to play it safe—let's make it a thrilling ride, one daring step at a time!

what will it cost you?

Fear of Failure Can Hold You Back from Living Your Best Life!

Key impacts on your Professional Life:

Missed Career Opportunities
- Women may avoid applying for promotions or new roles due to fear of inadequacy, leading to stagnation in their careers.

Limited Innovation
- A reluctance to take risks can stifle creativity, preventing women from proposing new ideas or solutions that could advance their careers or organisations.

Reduced Networking
- Fear can cause women to shy away from networking events or professional gatherings, limiting their connections and opportunities for mentorship.

Impaired Leadership
- Women may hesitate to take on leadership roles or speak up in meetings, which can undermine their visibility and influence in the workplace.

Financial Impact
- Avoiding risks can result in missed financial opportunities, such as salary negotiations or investments in personal development, affecting long-term financial growth.

what will it cost you?

Fear of Failure Can Hold You Back from Living Your Best Life!

Key impacts on your Personal Life:

Increased Stress and Anxiety
- The pressure to avoid failure can lead to chronic stress, anxiety, and even burnout, negatively impacting mental health.

Decreased Self-Esteem
- Constantly fearing failure can erode self-confidence, making women doubt their abilities and worth, both professionally and personally.

Strained Relationships
- The stress associated with fear of failure can affect personal relationships, leading to withdrawal or tension with family and friends.

Isolation
- Women might isolate themselves to avoid the risk of failure, leading to feelings of loneliness and a lack of support.

Limited Personal Growth
- Avoiding challenges out of fear can hinder personal development and the ability to learn from experiences, resulting in a less fulfilling life.

Self-Criticism

"Spend less time tearing yourself apart, worrying if you're good enough.

You are good enough.
And you're going to meet amazing people in your life who will help you and love you."
-Reese Witherspoon

Self-Criticism

The Bad Friend That Won't Leave

Self-criticism is that little voice in your head that seems to have an endless supply of negative feedback. It's like having a personal coach who only points out your flaws, never your strengths. This inner dialogue often focuses on perceived failures, mistakes, or shortcomings, leading to a constant cycle of doubt. Instead of celebrating achievements, self-critics tend to dwell on what they could have done better, creating a narrative that can feel both familiar and exhausting. It's that nagging feeling that no matter how hard you try, you're never quite good enough.

At its core, self-criticism can stem from a variety of sources, including societal pressures, past experiences, or even just a desire for perfection. For many, it's a way to motivate themselves, if they keep pushing, maybe they'll finally reach that elusive ideal. However, this often backfires. Instead of fostering growth, excessive self-criticism can lead to anxiety, low self-esteem, and even burnout. It's like trying to fuel a car with a leak in the petrol tank: no matter how much you pour in, you're always running on empty.

The tricky part about self-criticism is that it can be hard to recognise when it's happening. It can masquerade as a helpful critique or a drive for improvement, making it easy to overlook its detrimental effects. When self-criticism goes unchecked, it can create barriers to success and happiness. Recognising this pattern is the first step toward transforming that inner critic into a more supportive voice—one that encourages you to learn from mistakes rather than dwell on them. After all, everyone stumbles; it's part of being human.

Embracing a little self-kindness can go a long way in fostering resilience and growth.

One of the most insidious aspects of self-criticism is its ability to isolate individuals. When you're trapped in a cycle of negative self-talk, it can be difficult to reach out for support. You might feel like others wouldn't understand your struggles or that you'd be judged for not measuring up. This isolation can lead to feelings of loneliness and even depression, as the inner critic thrives on silence and self-doubt. The irony is that sharing our vulnerabilities can often lead to a sense of connection and relief—turns out, we're all battling our own inner gremlins!

Proceed with Caution
Comes with Side Effects

Self-criticism can be a sneaky little gremlin that creeps into the minds of professional women when they least expect it. You know the drill: you finish a big presentation, and instead of celebrating your success, you replay every little mistake like it's a highlight reel of your worst moments. Did you stutter? Forget a key point? Well, congratulations! You've just won the "Most Likely to Over-analyse Every Word" award. This habit not only steals your joy but also saps your confidence, making it harder to take on new challenges. Spoiler alert: that internal critic isn't always right!

Let's talk about the ripple effect of self-criticism. When you're constantly berating yourself, you might find your motivation taking a nosedive. It's hard to muster enthusiasm for that big project when you're convinced you'll just mess it up. You might even start avoiding opportunities altogether, which is like skipping dessert at a fancy restaurant because you're worried about calories—sure, it seems sensible, but you're really just missing out on the good stuff. And let's face it, nobody's winning awards for being the most self-deprecating person in the room!

The truth is, every professional woman has her own struggles—so why not bond over them instead of wallowing solo? Embracing a little self-compassion could be the secret ingredient to not just surviving, but thriving, in your work and life.

There is a Sweet Spot

Finding the sweet spot in self-criticism is all about striking harmony between giving yourself constructive feedback and showing a little self-compassion. Think of it like perfecting your favourite recipe: too much salt can ruin the dish, but just the right amount enhances the flavour. The goal is to recognise when your self-criticism is genuinely helping you—like spotting areas for improvement—versus when it turns into a damaging spiral of negativity. This sweet spot allows you to acknowledge mistakes without letting them define you, creating a space where you can grow and thrive without being overshadowed by self-doubt.
To discover this harmony, try practising mindful reflection. Instead of diving into harsh judgements after a setback, take a moment to step back and assess the situation. Ask yourself questions like, "What did I learn from this?" or "What can I do differently next time?" This shift in perspective turns self-criticism into a more constructive conversation, where the focus moves from blame to growth. You want to be your own supportive coach, not a relentless critic—because honestly, who needs someone shouting negative comments from the sidelines when you're already doing your best? Ultimately, finding this sweet spot is a journey, not a destination. It's all about regularly checking in with yourself and adjusting your internal dialogue as needed.

what will it cost you?

Self-criticism steals your joy!

Key impacts on your Professional Life:

Reduced Confidence
- Can erode self-esteem, making a woman doubt her abilities. This lack of confidence can lead to missed opportunities, such as applying for promotions or taking on challenging projects, ultimately hindering career growth.

Impaired Decision-Making
- A critical inner voice can lead to overthinking and indecisiveness. This can result in missed deadlines or poor choices, which may harm professional relationships and affect overall job performance.

Burnout and Stress
- Self-criticism often leads to increased stress and burnout, as individuals push themselves to unrealistic standards. This can result in absenteeism, decreased productivity, and long-term health issues, costing both the individual and their organisation.

Limited Risk-Taking
- Can shy away from taking risks or stepping outside her comfort zone. Can prevent from pursuing new ventures, exploring leadership roles, or engaging in entrepreneurial opportunities, ultimately costing her potential growth.

what will it cost you?

Self-criticism steals your joy!

Key impacts on your Personal Life:

Decreased Self-Esteem
- Constant self-criticism undermines self-worth, leading to feelings of inadequacy and impacting relationships with family and friends.

Increased Anxiety and Stress
- The pressure to meet unrealistic standards can heighten anxiety and lead to chronic stress, affecting mental and physical health.

Isolation
- A self-critical mindset may cause a woman to withdraw from social interactions, fearing judgment, which can lead to loneliness and weakened support networks.

Impaired Relationships
- Struggles with self-acceptance can affect how she interacts with others, potentially leading to conflicts and misunderstandings in personal relationships.

Negative Impact on Self-Care
- Self-criticism can lead to neglecting self-care routines and healthy habits, resulting in physical and emotional burnout and diminishing overall well-being.

Questions

Curiosity is a woman's
greatest ally;
the more we ask,
the more we discover
our strength and purpose."
-Tori G. Doyle

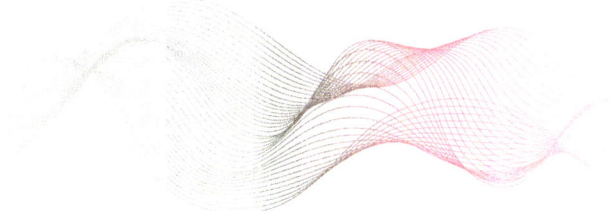

Questions

Asking the right questions ignites sparks that drives us forward.

Curiosity is a powerful force that propels women through life. It ignites the journey toward knowledge and experience, shaping who we are. Whether exploring new hobbies, cultures, or challenging the status quo, curiosity is our greatest ally. It opens doors to new perspectives and fosters meaningful connections, reminding us that every question can lead to something beautiful and transformative.

Meta questions, often seen as philosophical, are game changers in both work and life. They serve as the ultimate self-reflection tool, helping us dig deeper into our desires and choices. In meetings or decisions, asking, "Why am I here?" can lead to revelations that harmonise professional and personal lives.

In professional settings, meta questions challenge biases and assumptions. Asking, "What am I assuming about my abilities?" helps recognise our strengths. Research shows that self-awareness is linked to better career outcomes and leadership effectiveness (Goleman, 1998). By questioning our thoughts, we upgrade our mental software, navigating careers with confidence.

Questions like, "How do my past experiences shape my reactions today?" These questions enhance how we express feelings, whether in professional environments or personal interactions.

Embracing meta questions isn't just introspective; it's about taking charge of our stories and ensuring success in both professional and personal lives.

Once you've taken the time to explore these questions, remember that every insight and realisation brings you closer to understanding your true self. Embrace the clarity and confidence you've gained. Trust in your journey, knowing that you have the strength and wisdom to navigate whatever comes your way. You are capable, resilient, and deserving of success and happiness in all areas of your life. Keep asking questions, keep growing, and let your unique light shine brightly. You've got this!

Now, let's get a bit nerdy. In professional settings, meta questions can help you challenge those pesky biases and assumptions that tend to linger around like over used perfume. For instance, asking, "What am I assuming about my abilities?" can help you realise that maybe you're not giving yourself enough credit. Research shows that self-awareness is linked to better career outcomes and leadership effectiveness (Goleman, 1998). So, when you start questioning your own thoughts, it's like upgrading your brain's software, suddenly, you've got the tools to navigate your career with a lot more confidence.

On the personal side, meta questions can work wonders for your relationships. When you ask, "How do my past experiences shape my reactions today?" you're not just indulging in some deep introspection; you're actively improving how you communicate with others. Studies suggest that emotional intelligence—knowing yourself and understanding others—is crucial for healthy relationships (Goleman, 1995). So, whether you're trying to explain why you need a night off from socialising or just navigating family drama, these questions can help you articulate your feelings better. In the end, embracing meta questions isn't just about being introspective; it's about taking charge of your story and ensuring it's a bestseller.

PERFECTIONISM, HOW HAS IT COST YOU?

How have your perfectionist tendencies influenced the way you communicate with others, and what impact has that had on building trust and connection in your relationships?

In what ways has your pursuit of perfection led to missed opportunities for collaboration or creativity, both in your professional, business and personal connections?

PERFECTIONISM, HOW HAS IT COST YOU?

What specific instances can you recall where your perfectionism created tension or conflict in your relationships, and how did that impact?

How has the pressure you place on yourself for flawless outcomes affected your overall well-being and sense of fulfillment in both your work and personal life?

FEAR OF FAILURE, HOW HAS IT COST YOU?

What would be different in your life if you were to embrace failure as a stepping stone to success?

How might your perception of failure change if you viewed it as feedforward instead of a setback?

FEAR OF FAILURE, HOW HAS IT COST YOU?

What beliefs about failure have you inherited, and how might challenging these beliefs open new paths to success?

How would your confidence change if you celebrated small failures as part of your journey toward achieving your professional aspirations?

SELF-CRITICISM, HOW HAS IT COST YOU?

What would change in your life if you transformed self-criticism into self-encouragement?

What would your life look like if you treated yourself with the same kindness that you extend to others during difficult times?

THE ULTIMATE BURN BOOK FOR THE SUCCESSFUL WOMAN WITHIN

SELF-CRITICISM, HOW HAS IT COST YOU?

What positive qualities do you often overlook about yourself due to self-criticism, and how might acknowledging them impact your confidence?

How would your daily experiences shift if you approached challenges with curiosity instead of self-judgment?

-PART TWO-

SPIRITUALLY

"You are the creator
of your own reality."

-Esther Hicks

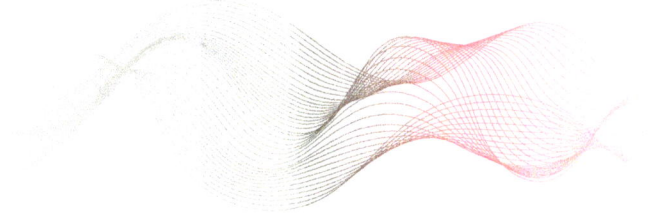

SPIRITUALLY

Visualisation

Unwoo Wooed It

The science behind visualising the act of burning a negative statement involves a combination of cognitive psychology and neuroplasticity. When you visualise this process, you're engaging in a mental exercise that can help re-frame your thoughts and emotions.

Here's how it works:

Cognitive Re-framing

Visualising the burning of a negative statement allows you to confront and transform those thoughts. By imagining the act of destruction, you create a symbolic release of the negativity attached to that statement. This can help diminish its hold over you, making it easier to replace it with a more positive affirmation.

Neuroplasticity

Our brains are capable of changing and reorganising themselves based on experiences. When you repeatedly visualise burning a negative thought, you're reinforcing new neural pathways that promote positive thinking. This means that over time, your brain can become wired to focus more on empowering beliefs rather than limiting ones.

Emotional Release

The act of visualising burning can also provide a sense of emotional catharsis. It allows you to express and release built-up feelings associated with the negative statement, which can lead to reduced anxiety and improved mental well-being.

In a ~~Nut~~ Brain Cell

Visualising the burning of a negative statement is a powerful technique or you can call it a ritual that leverages cognitive re-framing and neuroplasticity to help transform negative thoughts into positive ones, fostering a healthier mindset.

Now The Burning Question...
What is a Ritual?

Modern rituals are all about carving out a special moment in our busy lives that helps us reconnect with ourselves and our intentions. Think of them as little pockets of joy that remind us to pause, breathe, and appreciate the present. Whether it's lighting a candle while sipping your favourite tea or doing a mini dance party in your living room, these rituals can bring a sprinkle of magic to the mundane. Plus, they're a great excuse to wear those fuzzy slippers you've been saving for "a special occasion"!

How does the ritual of burning paper serve as a way to let go of negative thoughts and beliefs?

This metaphorical burning is like a mental spring cleaning. Once you've let go of those doubts, you'll feel lighter and ready to tackle your next big challenge. It's amazing how releasing negativity can ignite your confidence and help you show up in awesomeness in your professional and personal life!

Benefits of this Practice

How does the ritual of burning paper serve as a way to let go of negative thoughts and beliefs?

Emotional Release

You know that feeling when you write down all those negative thoughts and then just let them go? It's like a huge weight lifts off your shoulders! Burning those worries (metaphorically, of course) helps you ditch fears, self-doubt, and those annoying limiting beliefs that hold you back.

Symbolic Cleansing

This simple act can feel super empowering. It's like cleansing your space and your mind at the same time! You'll feel lighter and way more focused, ready to tackle your work with a fresh perspective.

Enhanced Focus

When you release all that negativity, it clears out the mental clutter. Hello, enhanced focus! You'll find yourself making better decisions and tapping into your creativity, both in your business and personal life.

Mindfulness

This ritual encourages you to be present and really reflect on your dreams and goals without all that negative baggage weighing you down. It's all about being in the moment!

Increased Confidence

Letting go of those shitty negative beliefs can seriously boost your self-confidence. You'll start chasing opportunities and challenges with a much more positive attitude.

By weaving this ritual into your life, you can create a more empowering and supportive mindset.

Take a Moment to Receive

Receiving support spiritually is incredibly important for women, as it can foster a deep sense of connection and empowerment. Tapping into our own strengths or seeking guidance from a higher power, whether that's God, the universe, or even the wisdom of a loved one can serve as a source of comfort and inspiration.

This spiritual connection can remind us of our inherent worth and resilience, especially during challenging times.
The meaning of this spiritual support can vary widely among individuals. For some, it may manifest as a sense of divine purpose or guidance, providing clarity and direction.
For others, it might involve feeling the presence of a loved one who has passed, offering emotional strength and reassurance.
This connection can be particularly crucial when women feel disconnected or overwhelmed.
By nurturing this spiritual aspect, they can find solace, rediscover their inner strength, and cultivate a more profound sense of belonging in the world.
Ultimately, connecting to something greater can help us as women navigate life's challenges with greater confidence and hope.

Flipping the Script Ready to Receive

So, here's the magic: flipping the script on negative statements can be a game-changer. When faced with a not so nice thought, instead of letting it drag you down, you can give it a little twist and find something positive. It's like a mental magic trick—poof! That negativity disappears, and suddenly you're looking at the brighter side.

Now, let's get a bit geeky for a second. This technique is rooted in cognitive re-framing, a psychological strategy that helps change how we perceive situations (Neff, 2003). By reframing our thoughts, we're not just slapping a smiley face on our problems; we're genuinely altering our mental landscape. This shift in perspective can boost our emotional well-being, making us more resilient when life throws curve balls.

Speaking of resilience, let's chat about neuroplasticity for a moment. Our brains are incredibly adaptable, kind of like that friend who can pull off any hairstyle (Doidge, 2007). When we practice flipping negative thoughts into positive ones, we're strengthening those neural pathways, creating a more flexible mindset. Each time you re-frame your thoughts, you're giving your brain a mini workout, and trust me, it loves the exercise!
Now, let's get a little serious. Regularly practising this mental flip can lead to long-lasting benefits like increased happiness and reduced stress (Fredrickson, 2001). It's not just about seeing the glass as half full; it's about building a habit of finding the silver lining in every situation. This mindset shift can enhance relationships, spark creativity, and even improve problem-solving abilities. So, when negativity creeps in, remember that you have the power to change the narrative.
You Got This!

Ready to Write Your Burn and Receiving Statements?

Get Comfy

Transforming negative statements into positives isn't merely a fun trick; it's a vital skill for professional and personal growth. By embracing cognitive re-framing and leveraging neuroplasticity, you can reshape your mindset and elevate your quality of life.

So go ahead—take that "I messed up" and turn it into "I'm learning!" Life's too short to dwell on the negatives when there's a world of positives just waiting to be uncovered!

Let's Start with your Burn Statement

Step One

Create Your Space
Find a comfortable and quiet place where you won't be disturbed. You can sit or lie down in a relaxed position. Dim the lights, play soft music, or light a scented candle if you wish. Set your phone to "Do Not Disturb" to minimise interruptions.

Step Two

Breathwork for Mental Clarity
Inhale deeply through your nose, expanding your abdomen. Exhale slowly through your mouth, emptying your lungs completely. Pay attention to the sensation of your breath and the rhythmic movement of your body.

Step Three

Reflect on Your Experiences
Burn Statement Only - Bring to mind a negative experience or belief related to your perfectionism, fear of failure or self-criticism.
Reflect on how it has cost you?
How does it make you feel?
Acknowledge its presence without judgement.

Step Four

Tune in to Your Inner Voice
Pause for a moment, and when you feel prepared, write a statement that reflects how your limiting beliefs have influenced your life.

Receiving Statement

Get Comfy Again

Step One

Create Your Space
Pop back into your comfortable and quiet place where you won't be disturbed. Sit or lie down in a relaxed position. Dim the lights, play soft music, or light a scented candle if you wish. Set your phone to "Do Not Disturb" to minimise interruptions.

Step Two

Visualisation Breathing
Inhale deeply through your nose, expanding your abdomen. Exhale slowly through your mouth, emptying your lungs completely.
Pay attention to the sensation of your breath and the rhythmic movement of your body.
As you inhale, visualise drawing in positive energy. As you exhale, release any tension or negative thoughts.

Step Three

Reflect on Your Experiences
Receiving Statement Only - Bring to mind a positive experience or belief related to your burn statement. Reflect on how it had added value to your life?
How did it make you feel?
Acknowledge its presence without judgement.

Step Four

Flip Your Script

Take a moment and when you're ready, write your receiving statement, flipping your burn statement to reframe into a positive one, ready to receive.

HINT: Take all the negative words and replace them with the opposite; positive words. Unworthy to Worthy, Weak to Empowered/Strong

Visualisation In Session

"Holding on is believing that there's only a past, letting go is knowing that there's a future."
— Daphne Rose Kingma

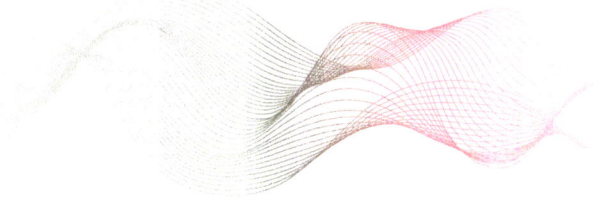

SPIRITUALLY

Visualisation In Session

It's time to burn this bi**h

This Visualisation exercise can be achieved in one of two ways: independently or with the assistance of a trusted friend who can guide you with the flame of freedom guided meditation script. *(Flame to Freedom guided meditation script found at the end of your book)*

Read through the step-by step instructions below first so you become more familiar with the process. When you feel comfortable, just start.

Step-by-Step Instructions

Step One

Find a Quiet Space
Just like before, choose a comfortable and quiet location where you won't be disturbed. This will help you focus fully on the exercise.
(Keep both your burn and receive statements close to you, if you need to read them)

Step Two

Get Comfortable
Sit or lie down in a relaxed position. Close your eyes if you feel comfortable to, and start your *visualisation breathing*

Inhale deeply through your nose, expanding your abdomen. Exhale slowly through your mouth, emptying your lungs completely.

Pay attention to the sensation of your breath and the rhythmic movement of your body.

As you inhale, visualise drawing in positive energy. As you exhale, release any tension.

Step Three

Visualise the Statement

Imagine you have a giant eye in your brain, your mind's eye. Now look at your negative statement written on a piece of paper. It's perfectly normal if you don't see the words; it may just come as the feeling of it. If you can, picture or feel it clearly, including the words and any emotions associated with it.

Step Four

Prepare to Burn

Visualise a flame, perhaps a candle or a campfire. Imagine bringing the paper with the negative statement close to this flame. Feel any tension or heaviness associated with the statement begin to lift.

Step Five

Burn the Statement

As you bring the paper closer to the flame, visualise it igniting and burning away. Watch the flames consume the paper, turning it to ash. Imagine the negative feelings dissipating with the smoke, leaving you lighter and freer.

Step Six

Replace with Positivity

Once the paper has turned to ash, take a moment to feel the release.

Take a moment for self-compassion. Now, visualise your receiving statement, your positive affirmation that counteracts the negative statement (eg. "I am capable and worthy"). Picture this new statement clearly in your mind.

Step Seven

Embrace the New Thought
Imagine the positive affirmation glowing brightly in your mind. Feel it being present to you through your own spiritual belief. Allow yourself to receive it with love and compassion and absorb its energy and strength filling you up.

Take a few more deep breaths, grounding yourself. When you're ready, gently open your eyes and take a moment to reflect on the experience.

a little side note

Rinse and Repeat as Needed
You can revisit this exercise whenever you feel that negative old friend pops in for a visit.
Regular practice can help reinforce positive thinking and diminish the impact of negativity.

Be patient with yourself; it may take time to fully internalise the new belief.

HINT: Feel free to journal or draw about your experience afterwards to solidify your insights.

Manifesting

"The universe is not outside of you. Look inside yourself; everything that you want, you already are."
— Rumi

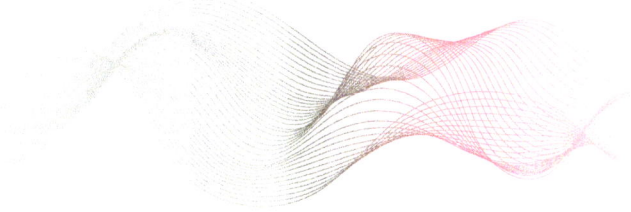

SPIRITUALLY

Manifesting

Bring it On!

Manifesting isn't just for dreamers with crystals and vision boards it's a powerful tool for women navigating the wild world of careers and personal lives. Think of manifesting as your GPS for success. You wouldn't head out on a road trip without google maps, right?

When you set clear intentions and visualise your goals, you're basically telling the universe, "Hey, this is where I want to go!" Plus, it beats aimlessly wandering around like a lost tourist in a new city. Now, let's be real, manifesting isn't about sitting on your couch in yoga pants and waiting for your dreams to come to you like pizza delivery.

You've got to put in the WORK! It's about aligning your actions with your intentions. So, while you're out there slaying in meetings and juggling personal commitments like a boss, keep that vision in your head. It's like having a secret weapon that makes even the toughest days feel a little more manageable (or at least a little more entertaining). And here's the kicker: when you manifest, you also attract a tribe of like-minded go-getters.
You'll find yourself surrounded by fierce women who are all about lifting each other up.
It's like hosting a fabulous brunch where everyone brings their best ideas instead of just mimosas.
So, go ahead, dream big, laugh at the challenges, and remember: the universe has your back if you're willing to put in a little elbow grease and add in some bloody good vibes!

Step Into Your Power

Ready to embrace your inner strength? Equip yourself with the tools you have now to conquer negative thoughts; it's time to seize the moment. Step over fear, on the other side is your untapped potential waiting for you!

Stepping back into your power and embracing the feeling of being "good enough" is a transformative journey that involves self-reflection, positive reinforcement, and mindfulness. By challenging negative beliefs, celebrating your achievements, setting boundaries, and practicing self-compassion, you can cultivate a deeper sense of self-worth.

Incorporating mindfulness techniques enhances your awareness and helps you stay present, reducing anxiety and fostering acceptance. Remember, this process is ongoing; it's about progress rather than perfection. Surround yourself with positivity, engage in personal growth, and be gentle with yourself as you navigate this path. Trust in your ability to reclaim your power and embrace your unique value. You are inherently worthy just as you are.

Take your First Steps Forward and Keep Going

Let's dive into setting your manifesting in motion with purpose driven actions that lead you toward your next adventure of growth.

Whenever those old limitations resurface, your burning ritual will be your trusted ally. It's a powerful practice that helps you keep the momentum going, allowing you to create new, positive mindset pathways. By embracing this ritual, you can transform setbacks into stepping stones.

To further support you on this journey, here are some amazing, creative, and proven tools you can incorporate. Whether it's journaling to clarify your intentions, visualisation techniques to see your dreams clearly, or surrounding yourself with uplifting women, these resources can help solidify your progress.

Remember, taking these steps is not just about reaching a destination; it's about enjoying the journey and discovering new aspects of yourself along the way. You have the strength and potential to create the life you desire.
Keep moving forward, one stepping stone at a time!

Your Creative Tools

Reflect and Expand

Grace With Gratitude
Cultivate gratitude through self-appreciation.

Personal Mantra
Replace self-criticism with a personalised mantra that affirms your worth.

Celebrate the Wins
Celebrate both big and small victories with joy.

Progress Over Perfection (7 Day Challenge)
Let's Step into the Freedom of "Good Enough"

You Are In Control Of Your Growth
Conquer your fears and step into growth.

Journal & Draw Out Your Truth
Self-Reflection Prompts creating success

Momentum Matrix
Pathway to Confidence and Success Framework

Flames To Freedom Guided Meditation

Grace and Gratitude

"Gratitude is the wine for
the soul. Go on,
Get drunk."

— Rumi

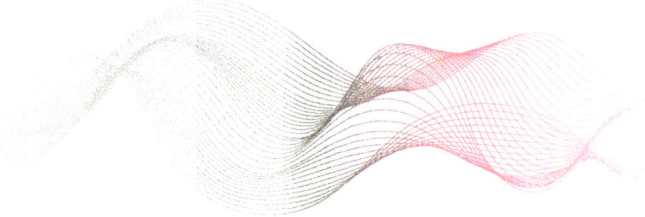

SPIRITUALLY

Grace and Gratitude

Bring it On!

Do it with Grace and Gratitude

You might be thinking, "Grace? Gratitude? Sounds great, but how do I keep my head above water when it feels like I'm drowning in obligations?"

Well, It's all about perspective. Imagine you're on a rollercoaster, there are ups and downs, twists and turns, but at the end of the ride, you can either scream in terror or throw your hands up and enjoy the thrill. Embracing grace means accepting life's chaos with poise, while gratitude acts as our safety harness, reminding us of the good stuff even when we're upside down.

So, how do we cultivate this magical combo? One way is through mindfulness. Picture yourself sipping your morning coffee; instead of scrolling through social media like a caffeinated zombie, take a moment to appreciate that warm cup in your hands. Research suggests that practicing mindfulness can significantly improve well-being and reduce stress (Kabat-Zinn, 2003). It's like giving your brain a spa day while you're at it!

Now, let's get a bit more serious. Living with grace and gratitude isn't just about feeling good; it's about resilience. Studies show that women who practice gratitude experience lower levels of depression and anxiety (Wood A M., 2010). When we focus on what we're thankful for, we're not just boosting our mood; we're also strengthening our mental fortitude.
It's like building a fortress around our hearts—one that can withstand life's storms.

Embracing grace and gratitude isn't just a feel-good mantra; it's a powerful tool for navigating the ups and downs of life. So let's don our invisible tiaras and strut through this world with confidence, knowing that every day offers a chance to find beauty—even when we're knee-deep in chaos. After all, a little grace and gratitude can turn even the most mundane moments into something magical. You've got this, and I'm right here cheering you on!

The Freedom Of "Good Enough"

Stepping into the mantra "I am enough" is like putting on a superhero cape—one that's made by Gucci or your favourite designer. For women in professional and personal worlds, this mindset transforms the ordinary into the extraordinary. Suddenly, you're not just checking off boxes on a to-do list; you're recognising your achievements, both big and small. That promotion? Celebrate it! That time you managed to keep your plants alive for a month? Worth a mini dance party! Acknowledging your successes, no matter how tiny, is the first step in building unshakeable confidence.

Embracing the chaos of life is another delightful perk. When you accept that mistakes are merely plot twists in your epic story, you can learn to laugh at the little hiccups.

Think of it as a comedy of errors—every misstep is just a chance to add a punchline. Allowing room for imperfections means you become more empathetic, not just to yourself but to others too. After all, we're all beautifully flawed humans navigating this wild ride together. So, whether you're stumbling through a presentation or mispronouncing "quinoa" at a dinner party, remember: it's all part of the charm! of YOU!

The Power of Connection

The magic happens when you connect with others, sharing your authentic self and fostering relationships that uplift everyone involved. Surrounding yourself with positivity, grace and gratitude creates a support network that feels like a warm hug. Celebrate those little victories, like getting through a Monday without spilling coffee on your shirt! Trust in your journey, knowing that you're more than enough just as you are. So go ahead, embrace your fabulous self, and let that inner light shine because the world needs your unique sparkle!

And if you need to remind yourself, give yourself a little GRACE along the way, with these powerful affirmations will help you fly.

I am grateful for my unique journey, embracing every step I take as a woman.

I celebrate my imperfections, knowing they contribute to my strength and identity.

I release the need for perfection and welcome the progress I make every day.

I appreciate my efforts, recognising they are more than good enough.

I choose to be kind to myself, honouring my worth beyond my achievements.

I am grateful for the support of those who love me just as I am, celebrating my authenticity.

I honour my feelings and allow myself to be beautifully human.

I embrace vulnerability as a source of strength and connection.

I embrace my flaws as essential parts of my true self.

I appreciate the empowering journey of self-discovery and self-acceptance.

I am thankful for my resilience in the face of self-doubt.

I choose grace over perfection, allowing myself to make mistakes.

I am grateful for the moments of joy that remind me life is not about perfection.

I appreciate my creativity, which flourishes when I let go of rigid expectations.

I honour my body and mind, accepting them as they are today.

I choose to practice self-compassion in my daily life.

I am the essence of beautiful.

Reflection Questions with Grace

What's a past failure that taught you something awesome, and how can you express gratitude for that experience while moving forward with grace?

How can you change your inner voice from harsh critic to supportive friend, celebrating your efforts with grace and gratitude when things don't go as planned?

I Am

"There's no prerequisites
to worthiness.
You're born worthy,
and I think that's a
message a lot of women
need to hear"
— Viola Davis

SPIRITUALLY

Your Personal Manifesting Mantra

I AM!

Negative thoughts and emotions can really take a toll on our bodies, especially for women. When we experience stress, anxiety, or unresolved emotions, our bodies can react in ways we might not even realise. Research shows that these negative feelings can lead to chronic issues like headaches, digestive problems, and even heart disease. The science behind this is rooted in the mind-body connection—our mental state can trigger physical responses. For instance, when we're stressed, our bodies release cortisol, which, over time, can lead to inflammation and other health problems if we don't find a way to manage those emotions (Goyal et al., 2014).

Now, here's where personal mantras come into play. A mantra is like a little cheerleader for your mental state. When you repeat a positive phrase to yourself, it can help shift your focus from those negative thoughts to something more uplifting. This practice isn't just fluff; it's backed by science! Studies have shown that mindfulness and affirmations can reduce stress and improve overall well-being (Keng., 2011). By embedding a personal mantra into your daily routine, you can create a mental space that fosters positivity and resilience, allowing you to process and release those negative emotions rather than hold onto them.

Incorporating a personal mantra into your life. It doesn't have to be anything fancy—just a simple phrase that resonates with you. Over time, this practice can help you rewire your brain, making it easier to let go of those heavy feelings and improving your mental and physical health. Remember, taking care of your emotional well-being is just as important as looking after your body, and small changes like these can lead to big improvements.

You have Positivity In YOU

Head to your peaceful spot and revisit a moment when you felt overwhelmed or stressed, whether at work or in your personal life.

Notice where you physically feel these emotions in your body.

Write down this emotion and draw a line to indicate where it resides in your body.

Repeat this process two more times until you have identified three significant emotions linked to your body.

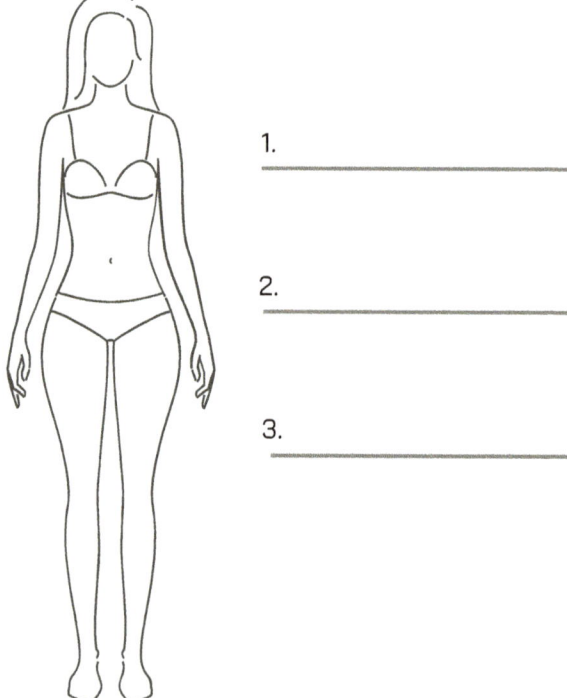

1. _____

2. _____

3. _____

Flip the Script

Replace any negative emotions with their positive counterparts. For example, swap feelings of unconfident with confidence, insecurity with safety, lack of love with love, and control with empowerment.
Let's change your mindset!
Incorporate these positive emotions into your personal mantra, recite it daily, keep it close, and check where these new feelings resonate in your body.

Negative to *Positive*

_____ to _____

_____ to _____

_____ to _____

Add your three positive words here

You NEW Personal Mantra

I am

_____ _____

and

_____

this is the woman I have always been.

Celebrating Wins

"Real queens celebrate
each other's wins, shining
brighter together."
-Tori G Doyle

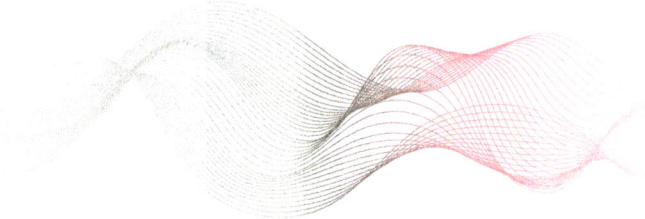

SPIRITUALLY

Celebrating Wins

WOO HOOOO!

Celebrating wins for women, whether in their professional or personal lives, is like throwing confetti at the everyday parade of life. It's a chance to acknowledge achievements, big or small, and to remind ourselves just how awesome we really are. Whether it's snagging that big promotion or finally mastering the perfect sourdough, these moments deserve a spotlight. Celebrating them not only boosts confidence but also encourages others to strive for their own successes. Plus, let's be real—who doesn't love a good reason to pop some bubbly?

Now, let's talk science! Celebrating victories triggers the release of feel-good chemicals in our brains, like dopamine and serotonin. These neurotransmitters are like the party planners of our neural pathways, promoting feelings of happiness and satisfaction.

On a broader scale, celebrating women's wins helps challenge societal norms and dismantle stereotypes. It creates a culture where women feel empowered to take risks and pursue their goals, knowing they have support. Celebrations encourage networking and mentorship, opening doors for future opportunities. So, the next time you or a fabulous woman in your life achieves something great, don't hold back on the confetti. After all, every win is a step toward a more equal and inspiring world.
Is there a little hesitation?

You know, it's funny how we women often hold back from sharing our wins, right? It's like we've been programmed to think that if we say, "Hey, I just nailed that presentation!" people will roll their eyes and mutter, "Oh great, here comes Ms. Show-off."

We're taught to be humble, but sometimes it feels like we're just one shiny trophy away from being labeled the office diva! So instead of strutting our stuff, we end up downplaying our achievements like, "Oh, it was nothing, really!" when deep down we're doing a little happy dance.

But here's the thing: sharing our wins with trusted people can be super important. It not only reinforces our own confidence but also inspires those around us. When we celebrate our victories, we create a ripple effect that can motivate others to pursue their goals. According to research by Dr. Tara Mohr in her book "Playing Big", women often underestimate their achievements, and sharing them can help shift that narrative. It's like saying, "Hey, I did this, and if I can, so can you!" It builds a supportive community where everyone encourages each other to shine.

Studies show that discussing achievements with trusted friends can help validate our feelings and experiences, making us feel more deserving of our success. In "The Confidence Code" by Katty Kay and Claire Shipman, they emphasise how women can boost their confidence by embracing their accomplishments rather than hiding them. It's not just about us; it's about lifting each other up and creating a culture of celebration.

So, let's break free from the shackles of modesty and start popping those confetti cannons! When we share our victories, we not only acknowledge our hard work but also pave the way for a more supportive environment where everyone feels empowered to celebrate their own wins. After all, if we don't celebrate ourselves, who will? Let's own our success, one shared story at a time!

The freedom of "good enough"

"You'll never do a whole lot unless you're brave enough to try."
— Dolly Parton

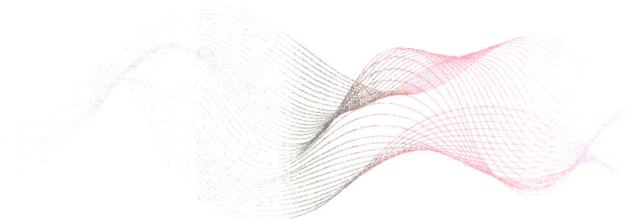

SPIRITUALLY

Let's Step into the Freedom of "Good Enough"

BLAHHHH, The pursuit of perfection can be exhausting. Imagine trying to juggle a career, business, personal life, and maybe even a side hustle while aiming for flawless execution. Spoiler alert: it's often more of a circus act than a walk in the park. But here's the good news! Embracing progress over perfection can be a game-changer for women navigating the professional world and personal goals. It's like trading in your high heels for a comfy pair of sneakers—much more practical and way less painful!

First off, focusing on progress allows women to break free from the shackles of unrealistic expectations. Have you ever spent hours obsessing creating the perfect bow on those perfect birthday invitations, only to see them folded up and shoved into a bag, your friends would have been just as impressed with any relatable version? When you prioritise progress, you give yourself permission to make mistakes or an uneven bow and learn along the way that good enough is enough.
This mindset not only boosts creativity but also fosters resilience. After all, every "oops" moment is just a stepping stone to the next big achievement.
The progress-over-perfection mantra is a fabulous antidote to burnout. Women often wear multiple hats—think CEO, mum, friend, and therapist all rolled into one. When you're constantly striving for perfection, it's easy to feel overwhelmed and underachieved. But when you celebrate small wins, you build momentum that energises you rather than drains you.
Imagine you finish a project and reward yourself with a cupcake instead of scrutinising every detail. Delicious, right?

In addition, this approach can lead to stronger connections in both personal and professional worlds. When you embrace authenticity and share your journey—flaws and all—you create a safe space for others to do the same. This vulnerability fosters trust and opens doors to collaboration and support.

Let's be real: nobody wants to work with a robot. People connect with real, relatable humans who are navigating the same choppy waters of life.

Now, if you're ready to dive into the world of progress, here's a fun 7-day challenge to get you started. Buckle up, because we're about to make progress your new best friend!

DAY ONE
Set Your Intentions

Write down three areas in your life where you feel pressured to be perfect (work, home, social media, etc.).
Under each one, jot down one small, manageable goal that represents progress instead of perfection.

DAY TWO
Tick, Job Done!

At the end of the day, reflect on what you accomplished, NOT PERFECT, good enough, no matter how tiny. Did you send that email? Boom! Celebrate with a dance break. Write down what you accomplished and how did you celebrate it?

DAY THREE
Share the Love

> Post a "progress, not perfection" update on social media. Share a project you're working on and invite others to share their journeys too.
> Bonus points for using a funny GIF

How did you shared the love?

Did sharing spark conversation?

DAY FOUR
Create a "Messy" Vision Board: Life Map

Grab some old magazines or print out some pictures and make a vision board of your life that embraces the chaos that you feel. Use images and words that represent you and the world around you, not perfection.
No self-judgement, do it fast; it'll look way more interesting! Just sit with your vision board for a moment and reflect on the feelings you have.

How did if feel? Was it difficult to make a mess?

DAY FOUR
Create a "Messy" Vision Board: Life Map

Did you feel as though you were making mistakes?

Could you see the beauty in your vision?

Did it feel free to just be good enough?

DAY FIVE
Forgive Yourself

Compose a letter to your current self, focusing on forgiveness for any self-limiting beliefs that have been clouded by fear. Show yourself compassion and kindness in the message. Seal it in an envelope to reflect upon in the future, and witness how much you have grown.

NOTES

DAY SIX
Try Something New

> Step out of your comfort zone!
> Book yourself in a workshop or course you have been putting of.
> Try a new hobby, like painting or cooking a new recipe, without the pressure of being a pro.
> Just have fun!

What did you do?

When you did it, did you enjoy the freedom of letting go of doing it perfect?

DAY SEVEN
Reflect and Share

> Reflect on your week. What did you learn about progress?
> Share your insights with a friend or in a group.
> You might inspire someone else to let go of perfection too!

Did learn something new about yourself?

How did your share your 7 day journey?

Did it inspire someone else?

Step Over Fear

"Above all, be the heroine
of your life. Not the victim."
—Nora Ephron

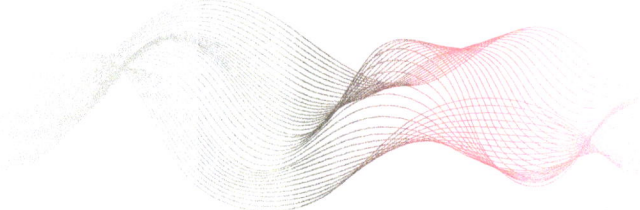

SPIRITUALLY

Step over Fear and Embrace the Unknown

Hope you are doing a happy dance!

Choosing progress over perfection isn't merely a trend; it's a lifestyle that can foster greater happiness, reduce stress, and add a lot of joy to your life. You've got this!

Remember, we all need some maintenance every now and then.
If you ever feel tempted to pursue perfection, pause and ask yourself, 'Is this truly helpful?' You already know what to do!
Take a moment to reflect on your past experiences. It's uplifting to see how far you've come. Even the smallest steps are still progress.
Hold on to these two beliefs:

- It's perfectly fine to fail; mistakes are simply part of my journey.
- Confidence grows from accomplishments, regardless of how messy, big, or small they may be.

These achievements help illuminate your positive spirit.

You're in Control of Your Growth

Let's face it: fear can feel like a four-legged creature sitting on your chest, making you second-guess every decision you make. For many women in the professional and personal worlds, that fear often stems from stepping outside their comfort zones. But what if I told you that embracing the unknown can lead to some pretty fantastic outcomes?

Let's dive into the positive effects of stepping over fear and breaking those comfort zone chains—complete with a sprinkle of science.

First up, let's talk about growth. When you step out of your comfort zone, you're essentially saying, "Hey, fear, not today!" According to a study published in the "Journal of Personality and Social Psychology", facing fears helps build resilience and adaptability (Bravery, 2020). Think of it like weightlifting for your brain. Each time you tackle a fear, like speaking up in a meeting or networking at an event—you're adding mental muscle. Before you know it, you'll be flexing your confidence like a bodybuilder in a gold bikini! Well, that might be a bit far.

Next on the agenda: creativity. Believe it or not, stepping outside your comfort zone can unleash your inner Picasso. Research from the "Creativity Research Journal" shows that new experiences can enhance creative thinking (Out-of-the-box, 2021).

So, when you try something new, like taking a pottery class or pitching a wild idea at work, you're not just risking embarrassment; you're also sparking your creative juices. Who knows? That awkward moment could lead to the next big innovation, or at least a funny story to tell at brunch.

Now, let's not forget the power of connection. Breaking out of your comfort zone often leads to meeting new people, and let's be real: networking can feel like a high school dance where everyone's just standing around. But when you take that leap, like joining a new professional group or volunteering, you open the door to potential friendships and mentorship. According to a study by the "Harvard Business Review", diverse networks can lead to increased opportunities and success (Networking, 2022). So, go ahead, strike up a conversation with that interesting stranger; they might just be your next business partner, or at least someone to share a laugh with!

Let's get a little scientific again. Stepping out of your comfort zone also triggers the release of dopamine, the "feel-good" hormone (Neuroscience for You, 2023). This brain boost can make you feel more energised and motivated.

So, each time you conquer a fear, you're not just winning the battle; you're also getting a mini dopamine party in your brain! Who knew tackling that dreaded presentation could come with a side of happiness?

In conclusion, stepping over fear and out of your comfort zone can lead to incredible benefits for women in both professional and personal lives. From building resilience and enhancing creativity to expanding your network and getting a delightful dose of brain chemistry, the rewards are plentiful. So, the next time you feel that familiar fear creeping in, remember: you've got the power to kick it to the curb. And who knows? You might just discover a whole new world of opportunities—and maybe even a great new friend or two along the way!

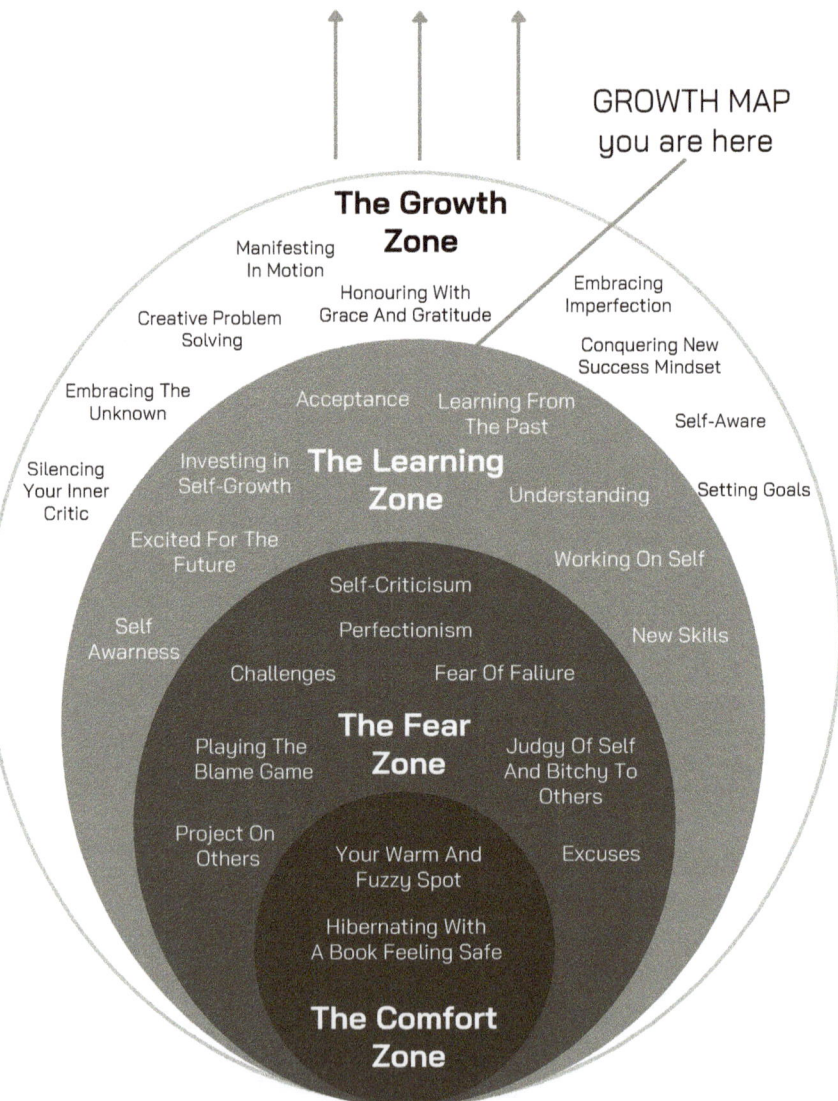

THE ULTIMATE BURN BOOK FOR WOMEN WHO DO IT ALL

You Are In Control

Fill In How You Want Your Sucess To Look Like On Your Growth Map

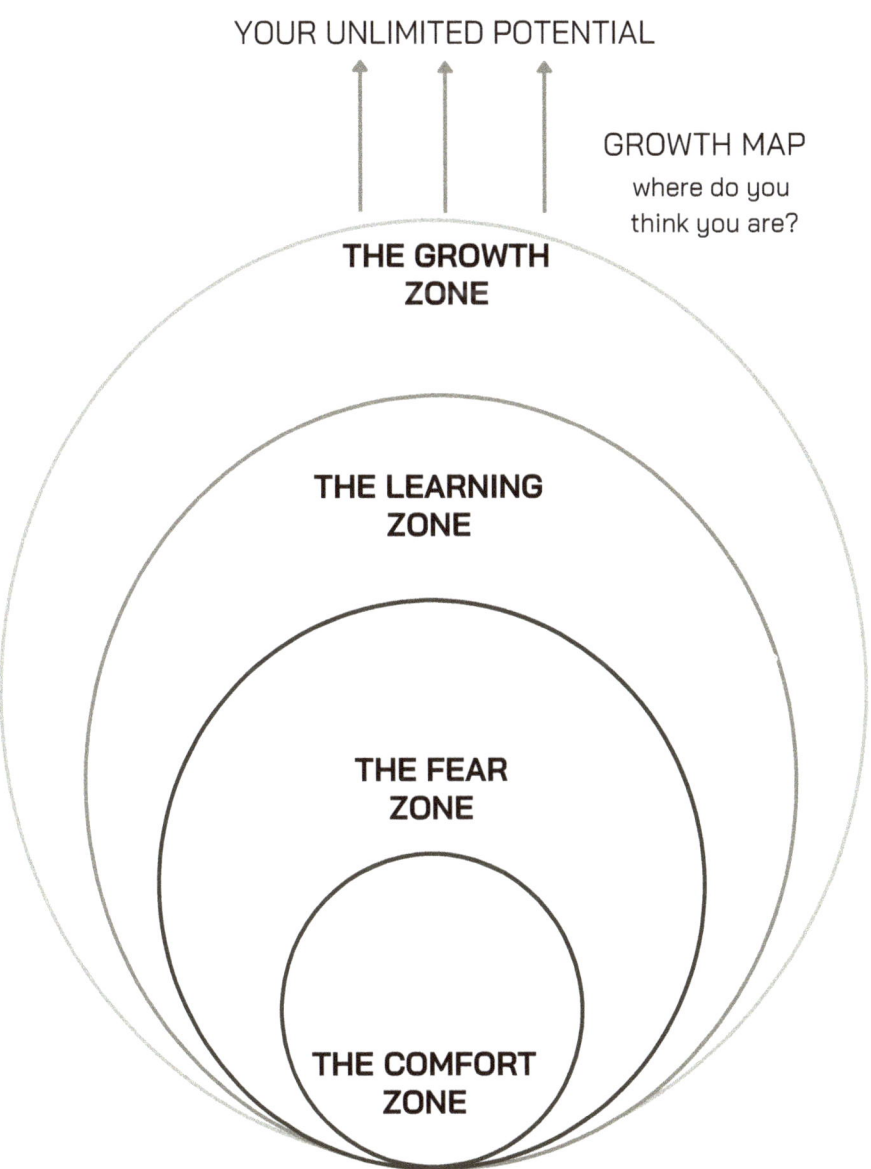

YOUR UNLIMITED POTENTIAL

GROWTH MAP
where do you think you are?

THE GROWTH ZONE

THE LEARNING ZONE

THE FEAR ZONE

THE COMFORT ZONE

THE GROWTH ZONE
You Have the Choice to Move

> Insight paves the way for new opportunities.
> You possess all the potential within you—have faith and take the leap!

How has staying in the fear zone cost you?

How did it feel, what emotions are coming up?

THE GROWTH ZONE
You Have the Choice to Move

> Insight paves the way for new opportunities.
> You possess all the potential within you—have faith and take the leap!

What would life look like when you put your manifesting in motion?

Where are you? Who is with you? What are you Feeling?

Journal and Draw

"1 found I could say things with colour and shapes that I couldn't say any other way - things I had no words for."
- Georgia O'Keeffe

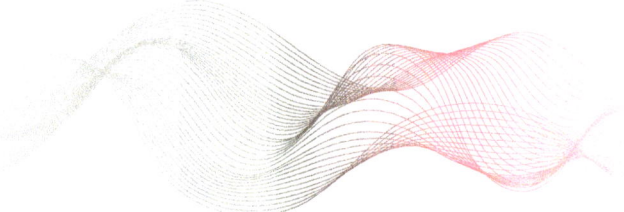

SPIRITUALLY

Journal & Draw Out Your Truth

trust your intuition
It's the first feeling that comes up, not 2nd, or the 3rd, 4th...

Journaling and drawing can be like your best friend who always knows how to help you sort through your feelings, without the judgement or need for a coffee date! When life throws its curve balls, scribbling down your thoughts or doodling your emotions can create a cosy little buffer between you and those overwhelming feelings. It's like having a personal therapist who's available 24/7 and only requires a pen and a notebook (or a sketchpad). Plus, you can do it in your PJs with a face mask on, talk about self-care! Now, let's get a bit science-y, shall we? Studies suggest that expressive writing can help reduce stress and anxiety, leading to improved mental health (Pennebaker & Chung, 2011). When you put your thoughts on paper, you're not just venting; you're also engaging in a cognitive process that helps you understand your emotions better. It's a bit like decluttering your mind. Drawing, on the other hand, taps into your creative side, which can release endorphins, those feel-good hormones that make you feel like you've just scored a free dessert at your favourite restaurant. Research shows that creative expression can lower cortisol levels, which means less stress and more chill vibes (Kaimal et al., 2016).

When you dive into journaling and drawing, you're engaging both sides of your brain in a delightful dance. The left brain, known for its logical and analytical prowess, often takes the lead in our daily lives, organising our thoughts and keeping us on track.

But let's be real, sometimes it needs a break from all that structuring and problem-solving! By journaling and drawing, you give that overworked left brain a well-deserved timeout. The right brain, the creative powerhouse, gets to shine, encouraging you to express yourself freely and intuitively. This harmony can not only enhance creativity but also help reduce anxiety as you switch gears from logical thinking to imaginative exploration (Hughes & O'Brien, 2020).

Moreover, engaging both hemispheres can foster neural connections that enhance overall brain function. Research suggests that integrating creative activities into your routine can lead to improved cognitive flexibility, allowing you to tackle problems from various angles (Dietrich, 2004). So, by indulging in a little journaling or doodling, you're not just giving your left brain a breather, you're also enhancing your brain's ability to adapt and thrive. It's like a mini-vaycay for your mind, where you can recharge and come back ready to tackle whatever life throws your way, armed with new insights and a lighter heart!

So, Gorgeous, next time you're feeling like a tidal wave of emotions is crashing down on you, grab that journal or sketchbook and start pouring your heart out (or doodling a cat wearing a tutu, no judgement here). Not only will you create a little emotional distance, but you'll also be boosting your mood and mental clarity. Plus, who doesn't want to unleash their inner artist?

Just remember, there's no right or wrong way to do it, so go ahead and let those feelings flow like a river of glitter and sparkles!

Reflection Journaling and Drawing Clarity Prompts

Grab Your Pretty Pens

HINT: If you find yourself thinking, "I'm not an artist," then it's time to step out of your comfort zone and start DRAWING!
This will give your analytical brain a well-deserved break.
Words are only an approximation, so don't hesitate to explore both mediums.

*Art is therapy for the soul,
healing that reaches beyond words.*

Self-Reflection
Write, Draw or both;
What are your strengths and achievements?

Self-Reflection
Write, Draw or both;
What makes you feel worthy?

Grace with Gratitude

Write, Draw or both:

How would it feel to embrace chanllenges with grace and how will this impact the people around you?

Grace with Gratitude
Write, Draw or both:
What are the things in your life you are grateful for?

Your Boundaries

Write, Draw or both:
How does it feel to Say No, protecting your time and energy?

Your Boundaries
Write, Draw or both:
If you haven't set boundaries, why?

Your Boundaries
Write, Draw or both:
What would life look like if you did?

Celebrate Your Wins

Write, Draw or both:
Your Success Timeline, the moments you had achieved something special in your life so far, big or small.

Surround Yourself with Positivity
Write, Draw or both:
Who are the supportive people who uplift you?

Surround Yourself with Positivity

Write, Draw or both:
How do you uplift the people around you?

Embrace Imperfection
Write, Draw or both:
What imperfections did you discover in yourself and life?

Embrace Imperfection
Write, Draw or both:
How did they shape you then and how you see them now that they are a part of being human and learning?

Investing in Personal Growth
Write, Draw or both:
What hobbies or courses that boosted your confidence?

Investing in Personal Growth

Write, Draw or both:
What is something you want to achieve in personal or professional growth?

Practice Mindfulness
Write, Draw or both:
How can you stay focused on the present moment instead of worrying about the past or future?

Visualise Your Best Self
Write, Draw or both:
What will life look like as the person you aspire to be?

Visualise Your Best Self
Write, Draw or both:
What will be the first thing you want to do?

Take Action
Write, Draw or both:
What would life look like stepping outside your comfort zone?

Take Action
Write, Draw or both:
How will it make you feel?

Be Kind to Yourself

Write, Draw or both:
How would you treat yourself with the same compassion you would offer a friend?

Be Kind to Yourself
Write, Draw or both:
How would it feel, to live without self-criticism?

TORI G DOYLE

As you reflect and navigate through the various paths of life, remember to pause and reconnect with this inner tranquillity.
Let this gift journaling and drawing be a life ritual, a sanctuary you can retreat to whenever the world feels overwhelming.
Surround yourself with positive influences and cherish moments of stillness and reflection.
In these moments, you'll find the strength to face any challenge and the clarity to make decisions that resonate with your true self.
May this journey be filled with growth, joy, and the unwavering belief in your own resilience.

-PART THREE-

PURPOSEFULLY

"When one door of happiness closes, another opens, but often we look so long at the closed door that we do not see the one which has opened for us"
-Helen Keller

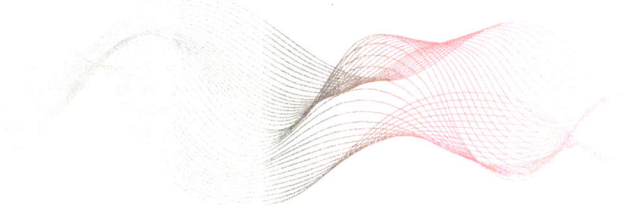

PURPOSEFULLY

Momentum Matrix

Pathway to Confidence and Success

So, you've armed yourself with all the tools for a new mindset and built a pathway to success with confidence. You're ready to take on the world, but then—bam! You hit a wall. It's like prepping for a marathon, training hard, and then finding yourself stuck at the starting line, unable to take that first step. This is a common experience, and it can be frustrating, but it's important to remember that feeling stuck doesn't mean you're failing.

Even with a solid foundation, life can throw unexpected challenges that make it hard to keep moving. You might find yourself overthinking decisions or second-guessing your abilities, even after you've done the work to silence that inner critic. This is where things can get tricky. It's essential to recognise that having the tools is just the beginning; it's the application of those tools that creates real change. Think of it this way: you can have all the ingredients for a fabulous dinner, but if you don't start cooking, you won't enjoy that delicious meal!

Creating momentum with purpose is key to breaking through that stuck feeling. When you take small, purposeful steps forward, you not only build confidence but also create a sense of progress. Research supports this idea, showing that even tiny victories can lead to a cascade of positive outcomes (Locke & Latham, 2002). Each step you take reinforces the neural pathways in your brain, making it easier to keep moving forward and less likely to revert back to old habits.

But let's be real: sometimes, the hardest part is just getting started. When you're feeling stuck, it's easy to let that momentum slip away. It's like trying to carry a heavy basket of laundry up the stairs—once you stop, it's a whole lot harder to start again. That's why it's important to establish routines or rituals that help you maintain momentum, even when motivation dips. Whether it's a morning walk, journaling, or a quick dance party in your living room, find what works for you!

Research in psychology shows that consistency is key to building habits and achieving your goals (Duhigg, 2012). When you create a routine that aligns with your purpose, you're setting yourself up for success, even on days when motivation is low. Remember, it's not about making giant leaps every day; it's about those small, consistent steps that eventually lead to significant change.

Another important aspect is accountability. Share your goals with a friend or join a community where you can support each other. Having someone to cheer you on (or gently nudge you when you're slacking) can make a world of difference. It's like having a best friend who reminds you of your strength and potential, especially on days when you might forget.

Finally, don't forget to celebrate your progress, no matter how small. Recognising your achievements reinforces that momentum and keeps you motivated. It's like throwing a little celebration every time you finish a project or reach a milestone. Trust me, you deserve it!

In the end, feeling stuck is just part of the journey. By keeping your focus on moving forward with purpose and maintaining momentum, you'll continue to build the life you want. So grab those tools, start cooking up your dreams, and remember: you've got this!

TORI G DOYLE

Momentum Matrix

A Little Help To Get You Moving

MOMENTUM MATRIX

Pathway to Confidence and Success

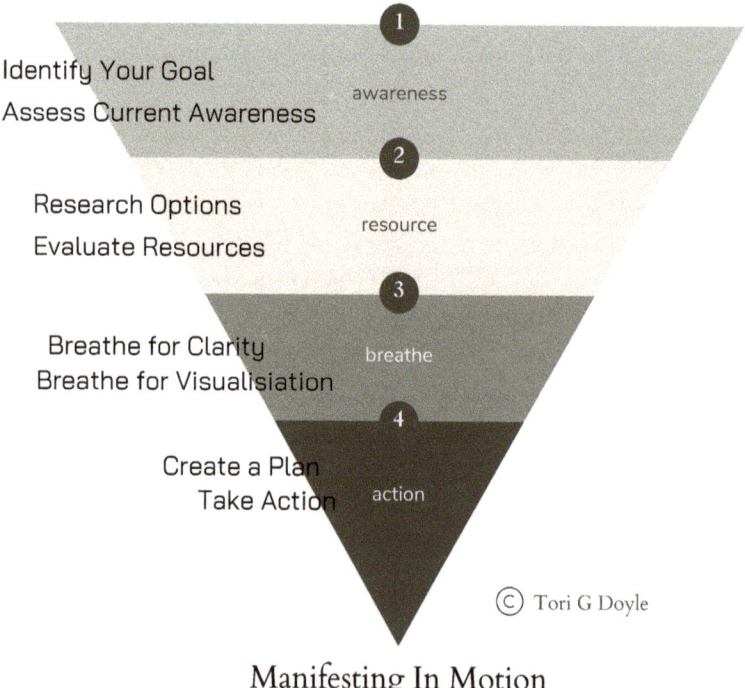

Manifesting In Motion

Momentum Matrix

Pathway to Confidence and Success

Navigating the world can be especially challenging for women who grapple with fear of failure, self-criticism, and perfectionism. The Momentum Matrix offers a refreshing approach to tackling these hurdles through a simple yet powerful four-phase process. This matrix isn't just a tool; it's a supportive framework designed to help women not only recognise their potential but also act on it with confidence.

Awareness is the first step in this trans-formative journey. It invites women to look inward and assess what they truly want to expand upon in their lives. Many times, fear of failure can cloud our vision and make us doubt our abilities. By cultivating awareness, women can identify their strengths, passions, and areas that need growth. This self-reflection is crucial—it allows them to visualise a clearer picture of their goals and the potential they possess. It's about shedding the layers of self-doubt and recognising that they can achieve what they desire.

Next comes the phase of Resources. Here, the idea is to harness the power of three. Women are encouraged to find three resources, be it books, mentors, or online courses—that resonate with their goals. If the first trio doesn't quite hit the mark, they can simply pivot to the next set. This approach not only emphasises exploration but also helps in minimising feeling overwhelm. Having a curated list of resources makes the journey feel more manageable and less daunting. It transforms the process of learning from a chore into an exciting adventure.

Now, let's talk about the power of breath. Breathing isn't just about oxygen; it's about creating space for clarity and calm. The first way to breathe involves taking a moment to pause and seek answers within. When self-criticism kicks in, taking a deep breath can provide the clarity needed to counter those negative thoughts. The second way to breathe focuses on visualisation. By actively picturing success, women can shift their mindset from one of fear to one of possibility. This dual approach to breathing is essential; it cultivates a sense of peace while fueling motivation.

Finally, we reach the phase of Action. This is where the magic happens. After gaining awareness, gathering resources, and breathing through the process, it's time to take tangible steps toward the goals. Action is often the most challenging part, especially for those who struggle with perfectionism. However, the Momentum Matrix encourages women to see action as a journey rather than a destination. Every small step taken is progress, and every misstep is a lesson learned. This shift in perspective helps to reduce the fear of failure, transforming it into an opportunity for growth.

The beauty of the Momentum Matrix lies in its ability to create a clear pathway for manifesting desires. By breaking down the journey into these four approachable phases, women can see that they have the power to shape their own narratives. Each phase builds on the last, providing a structured yet flexible framework that adapts to individual needs and circumstances.

As women engage with the Momentum Matrix, they begin to realise that they are not alone in their struggles. The process fosters a sense of community and support, allowing women to share their journeys and learn from one another. This camaraderie can be a game-changer, reinforcing the belief that confidence and success are not just for the chosen few, but for everyone willing to embark on this journey.

Ultimately, the Momentum Matrix is about empowering women to embrace their potential and step into their greatness. By equipping them with the tools to overcome fear, self-criticism, and perfectionism, it paves the way for a more confident and fulfilling life. Women are not just encouraged to dream; they are inspired to act, creating a ripple effect of positivity that extends far beyond themselves.

So, if you find yourself struggling with self-doubt or perfectionism, consider giving the Momentum Matrix a try. It's more than just a process; it's a revolution of self-empowerment that can help you manifest your goals and navigate the path toward success with renewed confidence.

Awareness: Unwrapping the Gift of Knowing

Awareness is one of those things that sneaks up on you, kind of like realising you've been mispronouncing "quinoa" for years. It's all about what we know, what we've experienced, and sometimes, what we think we know but really don't. People often say, "I've lived a sheltered life," like it's some kind of adorable excuse for not knowing how to parallel park. But hey, we only know what we know, right? Awareness is like that one friend who always knows the latest gossip and somehow manages to spill the tea without burning anyone.

Expanding our awareness is a bit like upgrading from an old flip phone to the latest smartphone. Suddenly, there's a whole new world of possibilities, and no, I'm not just talking about better selfies. Life experiences are the key here. They're like apps we download to make life a little more interesting and, occasionally, a little more complicated. Whether it's travelling to a new country or just trying sushi for the first time, each experience pushes the boundaries of what we know.

Curiosity is the fuel that propels us toward greater awareness. It's that inner voice that whispers, "What if?" or sometimes shouts, "Why on earth would anyone do that?" Asking questions is how we get the answers that expand our world view. Some questions are small, like "Why is the sky blue?" and some are mind-blowing, like "Is there intelligent life out there?" Spoiler alert: we're still working on that one.

But let's face it, awareness isn't always comfortable. Sometimes it feels like that awkward moment when you realise you've been walking around with spinach in your teeth. It can be a little embarrassing to discover just how much we don't know. Yet, that's the beauty of it—embracing the awkwardness and learning from it. After all, nobody ever said that becoming more aware was going to be all sunshine and rainbows.

As we grow more aware, we start to see the world in a different light. It's like putting on a pair of glasses and realising trees have individual leaves, and not just blobs of green. Our perceptions shift, and suddenly things that seemed insignificant before it stood out like a sore thumb. You might start noticing patterns in human behaviour or understanding complex issues that once seemed out of reach. It's like turning on a light in a dim room, everything becomes clearer.

Of course, awareness isn't a destination. It's more like an ongoing journey, with plenty of detours and unexpected roadblocks along the way. But that's what makes it exciting. Every twist and turn offers a chance to learn something new and add another layer to our understanding. It's a bit like binge-watching a TV series and getting hooked on the plot twists.

In this journey, it's important to keep a sense of humour. Sometimes the things we become aware of can be downright ridiculous, and laughing at ourselves is part of the process. After all, nobody wants to be the person who takes life too seriously. Awareness can be fun, like discovering that your pet has been judging you this whole time.

Ultimately, being aware means being present, open, and willing to learn. It's about embracing the unknown and diving headfirst into the sea of experiences life has to offer. So, let's keep our eyes wide open, ask those burning questions, and maybe, just maybe, discover something truly amazing about the world, and ourselves.

Breathe Two Ways

Breathing is often taken for granted, yet it's our lifeline. Most of us breathe without thinking about it, but did you know there are two primary ways to breathe? There's the chest breath, which is quick and shallow, and then there's the diaphragmatic breath, which is deep and calming. By consciously choosing to breathe deeply, we can tap into a more relaxed state, crucial for our overall well-being. It's like switching from a buzzing bee to a gentle breeze—much more pleasant!
The beauty of diaphragmatic breathing is that it activates our parasympathetic nervous system, which helps us chill out. This technique can be especially beneficial for women who often juggle numerous responsibilities. When we breathe deeply, we send signals to our body that it's okay to relax, helping us to better manage stress. So, if you ever find yourself feeling overwhelmed, just remember: you have the power to breathe your way to calmness.

To help you switch from that frantic chest breath to a soothing diaphragm breath, try this: find a comfortable seated position and place one hand on your chest and the other on your belly. Take a deep breath in through your nose, allowing your belly to rise while keeping your chest still. Exhale slowly through your mouth, feeling your belly fall. Do this for a few minutes and feel the difference. It's like giving your body a little hug from the inside!

Focus on the Breath for Answers

When life throws questions your way, sometimes the best answers come from within. Focusing on your breath can help you tap into your natural intuition, allowing you to connect with your inner self. Women have a unique ability to sense things intuitively, but often the noise of daily life drowns out that voice. By centering your breath, you create space for clarity and insight.

Taking a moment to breathe and reflect can provide perspective on any situation. It's like hitting the pause button on a chaotic movie; suddenly, you're able to see the plot twists more clearly. When you focus on your breath, your mind quiets down, and that inner wisdom can shine through. Whether you're facing a tough decision or just need some clarity, your breath is a reliable guide.

To engage in this practice, find a quiet spot where you won't be disturbed. Close your eyes and take a few deep breaths, inhaling through your nose and exhaling through your mouth. As you breathe, ask yourself the question you need clarity on. Focus on your breath and allow any thoughts or feelings that arise to flow without judgement. Trust that your intuition will lead you to the right answer.

Focus on Breath to Help Regulate Anxiety

Anxiety can feel overwhelming, but focusing on your breath can act as a powerful tool for regulation. When anxiety strikes, our breath often becomes shallow and rapid, which only exacerbates those feelings. By consciously shifting to deep, steady breaths, we can help ground ourselves and regain control. It's like finding your way back to shore after being tossed around in a stormy sea. Breath-work can create a calming effect on both the mind and body. It lowers heart rates, reduces stress hormones, and increases feelings of safety and security. For women, who often carry the weight of multiple roles, this practice can be a game-changer. By incorporating breath-work into your daily routine, you can build resilience against anxiety and enhance your overall emotional well-being.

To practice breath regulation, sit or lie down in a comfortable position. Inhale deeply through your nose for a count of four, hold for a count of four, and then exhale slowly through your mouth for a count of six. Repeat this cycle several times, allowing your body to relax with each breath. You'll soon feel a sense of calm wash over you, much like sinking into a warm bath after a long day.

Visualise Experiences and Life Goals

Visualisation is a powerful technique that can help you manifest your dreams and goals. When combined with focused breathing, it becomes even more effective. By calming your mind and concentrating on your breath, you create a fertile ground for your aspirations to blossom. It's like watering a plant; your goals need that nourishment to grow and thrive.

Breath-work helps to clear the mental clutter, allowing you to visualise your desired future in vivid detail. Whether you're aiming for a career change, personal development, or improving relationships, visualising these goals while breathing deeply can make them feel more attainable. It's all about creating a mental movie where you're the star, and the possibilities are endless.

To start visualising your goals, find a quiet space and get comfortable. Close your eyes and take a few deep breaths, letting your body relax with each exhale. Once you feel centred, picture yourself achieving your goal.
What does it look like? How does it feel?
Try to engage all your senses in this visualisation. Breathe into this image, allowing it to settle into your mind.
Repeat this practice regularly, and you may find it easier to move toward your aspirations.

MOMENTUM MATRIX
Pathway to Confidence and Success

1. awareness
2. resource
3. breathe
4. action

© Tori G Doyle

Manifesting In Motion

How to Use the Momentum Matrix
Step 1: Awareness

Identify Your Goal
- Find a quiet space where you can think without interruptions.
- Ask yourself, "What do I truly want to achieve?" Consider both professional and personal aspects.

Write down your goal in a clear and specific manner. For example, instead of " I want to help 50 more clients by...," or "I want to be healthier by...," write "I want to run a 5k in under 30 minutes by the end of the year."

Assess Your Current Awareness
- Reflect on what you know about this goal.
- What skills or knowledge do you already possess?
- Write down your thoughts, feelings, and any beliefs related to this goal. Consider questions like:
- What excites me about this goal?
- What fears or doubts do I have?
- What past experiences might influence my journey?

This awareness will serve as a foundation for your journey.

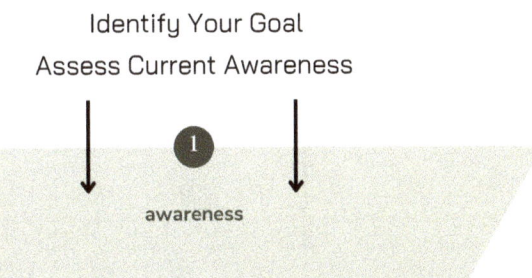

How to Use the Momentum Matrix
Step 2: Resources

Research Options
Start by brainstorming a list of potential resources. Think broadly.

- Books: Search for recommended titles in your area of interest.
- Website: Look for reputable blogs, online courses, or organisations that specialise in your goal.
- Podcasts: Identify podcasts that feature experts or success stories related to your goal.
- Courses: Explore online platforms for relevant classes.
- Mentors: Consider reaching out to individuals who have achieved similar goals.

Evaluate Resources
- Review your initial list of resources. Choose three that stand out based on your interests and needs.
- If these resources don't provide enough information or inspiration, discard them and search for the next set of three.

Take notes on what you find in each resource. Highlight key insights, strategies, or tips that resonate with you.

Research Options
Evaluate Resources

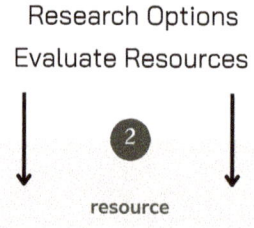

resource

How to Use the Momentum Matrix
Step 3: Breathe

Breathe for Clarity
- Set aside time for a quiet meditation session. Sit comfortably with your three resources nearby.
- Close your eyes and take several deep breaths. Inhale deeply through your nose, hold for a moment, and exhale slowly through your mouth.
- Focus your mind on the goal you've identified. Ask yourself, "What is the best way forward?" Allow your thoughts to flow without judgement.
- After a few minutes, open your eyes and write down any insights or ideas that emerged during this time.

This could include new perspectives or steps you hadn't considered.

Breathe for Clarity

How to Use the Momentum Matrix
Step 3: Breathe

Breathe for Visualisiation
- With your goal and insights in mind, find a comfortable position. Close your eyes again.
- Visualise or feel yourself successfully achieving your goal.
- Picture or feel the environment, people, and feelings associated with this success.
- As you visualise, breathe deeply, immersing yourself in the experience.
- Feel the joy, pride, and satisfaction of reaching your goal.
- After visualising, jot down the emotions and images that stood out to you.
- This will reinforce your motivation and commitment.

HINT: It's totally normal to struggle with visualisation. If that happens, just go with your gut instinct! Tune into how you're feeling and notice where that sensation sits in your body.

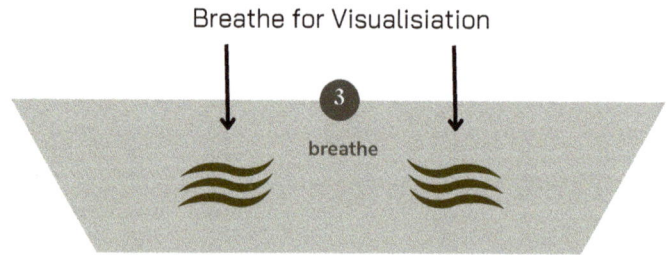

TORI G DOYLE

How to Use the Momentum Matrix
Step 4: Action

Create a Plan
Transform your insights into practical steps. Use the following structure as a guide: (feel free to adjust it to fit your timeline; it can span 2 to 3 months before or after your term goals).

- Short-Term Goals: Identify what you can achieve in the next week or month.
- Medium-Term Goals: Outline what you wish to accomplish in the next three to six months.
- Long-Term Goal: Define your ultimate goal and set a timeline for achieving it.
- Write your plan in a format that works for you, such as a table, bullet points, or a mind map.

Take Action
- Start with the first task on your list. Set a specific date and time to work on it.
- Use tools like calendars, to-do lists, or project management apps to stay organised and track your progress.
- Celebrate small wins along the way to keep your motivation high.

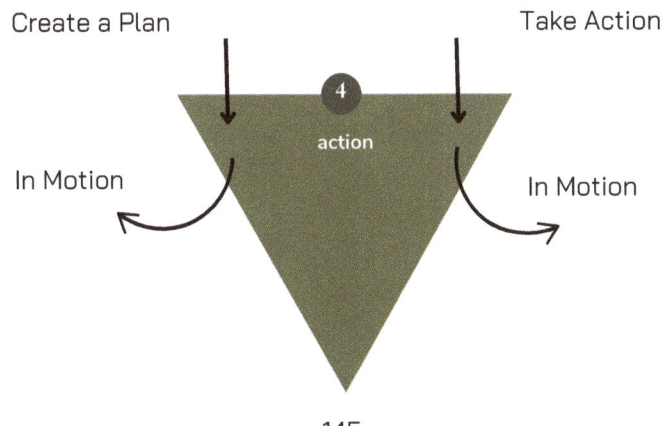

How to Use the Momentum Matrix

Reflect and Adjust

Schedule regular check-ins (weekly or monthly) to review your progress.
Ask yourself:
- What has worked well so far?
- What challenges have I faced?
- Do I need to adjust my plan or seek new resources?
- Make necessary adjustments to your action plan based on your reflections.
- Stay flexible and open to change as you progress toward your goal. (It doesn't need to be perfect)

By following these detailed steps in the Momentum Matrix, you can effectively transform your awareness into actionable steps.
This structured approach will empower you to build confidence, leverage resources, and take decisive actions toward achieving your professional and personal goals.

CASE STUDIES

Meet Sarah

Sarah is a 32-year-old personal trainer living in Sydney, Australia. With a passion for fitness and a strong commitment to helping others, she specialises in creating personalised workout programs that cater to her clients' specific goals. Currently, Sarah aims to expand her client base from 10 to 15 clients within the next six months. She believes that by reaching more people, she can have a greater positive impact on her community's health and fitness. Sarah is dedicated to inspiring others and fostering a supportive fitness culture in her local area.

Step 1: Awareness

Identify Your Goal
Sarah found a quiet space in her home gym, ensuring she would not be interrupted. She sat down with a notebook and a pen, ready to reflect on her aspirations.

- She asked herself, "What do I truly want to achieve?" After considering her desire to help others and grow her personal training business, she decided that her primary goal would be to increase her client base significantly.

- She articulated her goal clearly: "I want to increase my client base from 10 to 15 clients by March 2025." This specific target gave her a clear focus for her efforts.

Assess Your Current Awareness
To better understand her starting point, Sarah reflected on her current knowledge and skills related to her goal. She recognised that she had strong qualifications and experience as a personal trainer, as well as good communication skills that helped her connect with clients.

Sarah wrote down her thoughts, feelings, and beliefs surrounding her goal:
- Excitement: The prospect of helping more people achieve their fitness goals excited her, as she loved making a positive impact on others' lives.

- Fears and Doubts: She felt nervous about managing additional clients and worried about providing the same level of attention and care to each individual.

- Influences from Past Experiences: Sarah recalled successful experiences running small group sessions, which boosted her confidence in her ability to handle more clients.

Step 2: Resources

Research Options
Sarah began her resource search by brainstorming a variety of tools and materials that could help her grow her client base. She considered:
- Books: Comprehensive guides on managing and marketing a personal training business.
- Websites: Fitness blogs that offer tips on client engagement and marketing strategies.
- Podcasts: Features interviews with successful personal trainers sharing their experiences and strategies

- Courses: Online courses focusing on marketing skills specifically tailored for personal trainers.
- Mentors: Reaching out to a local trainer who had successfully expanded her client base for advice and potential collaboration.

Evaluate Resources

After compiling her list, Sarah carefully reviewed each resource to determine which would be the most beneficial for her goals.
She selected three standout options:
1. Book: For Personal Trainers - for foundational knowledge on running a training business effectively.
2. Online Course: A marketing strategies course aimed at personal trainers, focusing on social media and client acquisition.
3. Podcast: The latest episodes of a PT Show that featured practical advice from industry leaders.

Sarah took detailed notes while exploring these resources, highlighting key insights and strategies that resonated with her, such as:
- Effective social media strategies for showcasing client progress.
- Tips on building a referral network through existing clients.
- Ideas for community engagement through free classes or workshops.

Sarah laid a solid foundation of knowledge and strategies that would guide her actions in the next steps of her journey to expand her client base.

Through this awareness phase, Sarah established a solid foundation for her journey. She clarified her specific goal and reflected on her existing strengths and challenges, setting the stage for the next steps in the Momentum Matrix.

Step 3: Breathe

Breathe for Clarity
Sarah recognised the importance of taking time to reflect and gain clarity. She scheduled a quiet meditation session at home, ensuring she wouldn't be disturbed.

With her three selected resources she had read and listen to, the book, the online marketing course, and the podcast. She created a serene atmosphere by dimming the lights and lighting a candle.
- She sat comfortably, closed her eyes, and took several deep breaths, inhaling deeply through her nose, holding for a moment, and then exhaling slowly through her mouth.
- As she focused on her goal of increasing her client base, she asked herself, "What is the best way forward?" Allowing her mind to wander freely, she let go of judgement and simply observed her thoughts.
- After about ten minutes, Sarah opened her eyes and began to jot down insights that came to her during the meditation. She realised that she needed to: Focus on building community relationships to draw in clients.

Offer introductory sessions or workshops to showcase her training style and connect with potential clients.

Breathe for Visualisation
With renewed clarity, Sarah took another moment to visualise her success. She found a comfortable position, closed her eyes again, and imagined herself hosting a lively outdoor fitness class.

- She envisioned a diverse group of individuals—people of different ages and fitness levels—participating enthusiastically. Sarah could feel the energy and excitement in the air as everyone engaged with her guidance.

- As she immersed herself in this visualisation, she focused on the emotions of joy and fulfilment that came with helping others achieve their fitness goals.

- After several minutes of visualisation, Sarah opened her eyes and quickly drew and wrote down the vivid images and strong emotions she had experienced. She noted how fulfilling it felt to see others succeed and how this reinforced her commitment to her goal.

Through this breathing and visualisation process, Sarah gained deeper insights and renewed motivation to move forward with her plans for expanding her client base.

Step 4: Action

Create a Plan
With her insights and motivations clearly defined, Sarah developed a structured action plan to guide her efforts in expanding her client base.

She broke it down into specific goals:

Short-Term Goals (Next month)
- Host a free outdoor fitness class in a local park to attract potential clients.

Schedule this event for the first Saturday of the month to allow for adequate promotion.

Medium-Term Goals (Next three months)
- Launch a social media campaign showcasing client transformations and testimonials. This would include regular posts on Instagram and Facebook, highlighting success stories and fitness tips.
- Collaborate with local businesses (like health food stores or yoga studios) to cross-promote services and potentially host joint events.

Long-Term Goals (Next six months)
- Increase her client base from 10 to 15 clients by implementing referral incentives for existing clients.
- Conduct regular community workshops to establish herself as a fitness expert.

Take Action
Sarah immediately set to work on her first task: organising the outdoor fitness class. She created an event page on social media and started promoting it through her channels, encouraging her current clients to invite friends.

To stay organised, she utilised a digital calendar to schedule her marketing activities and client follow-ups. She set reminders for:
- Posting on social media three times a week.
- Reaching out to local businesses for potential collaborations.
- Sending personalised invitations to her existing clients for the outdoor class.

After the class, Sarah celebrated small wins, such as positive feedback from participants and gaining three new clients who expressed interest in personal training sessions.

Reflect and Adjust

After one month, Sarah took time to reflect on her progress. She scheduled a check-in session with herself to assess what was working and what needed adjustment.

She asked herself:
- What has worked well? (The outdoor class successfully attracted new clients, and her social media posts received positive engagement.)

- What challenges have I faced? (She noticed that balancing marketing tasks with training sessions was more time-consuming than anticipated.)

- Do I need to adjust my plan? (Yes, she realised she needed to dedicate specific hours each week solely for marketing activities to ensure consistency.)

Based on her reflections, Sarah adjusted her action plan by allocating two hours every Wednesday evening specifically for marketing efforts. She also decided to automate some social media posts to save time, allowing her to focus more on training and client interactions.

By following these structured steps in her action plan, Sarah was able to take decisive actions toward her goal of expanding her client base, reflecting on her progress, and making necessary adjustments to stay on track.

As of today, Sarah is making positive strides toward her goal of increasing her client base from 10 to 15 clients. She recently hosted a successful outdoor fitness class, which attracted several new participants and resulted in three new clients expressing interest in personal training sessions. Her social media campaign is also gaining traction, with increased engagement from potential clients.

Sarah has dedicated specific hours each week for marketing activities, which has helped her balance client training and outreach efforts more effectively. Her proactive approach, combined with her passion for fitness and community engagement, puts her on a promising path toward achieving her goal. Overall, she is motivated and optimistic about the progress she is making. She is also smashing Progression over Perfection!

Meet Emily

Emily is a 43-year-old entrepreneur based in Australia, where she runs a thriving social media marketing business. Known for her creativity and strategic thinking, Emily has built a loyal client base and gained recognition in her field. However, despite her professional success, she has been grappling with feelings of burnout and a lack of work-life "balance". Emily's passion for travel has taken a backseat to her growing list of client demands, leaving her yearning for more personal freedom. Determined to change her situation, she embarked on a journey to reclaim her time and explore the world, using the structured approach of the Momentum Matrix to guide her toward achieving her goal of harmonising work and adventure.

Step 1: Awareness

Identify Your Goal
Emily took time to find a quiet space in her home office, away from distractions. She asked herself, "What do I truly want to achieve?" After reflecting on her current situation and feelings of burnout, she articulated her goal: "I want to create a work schedule that allows me to travel for at least three weeks a year without compromising my business." This clarity gave her a specific target to aim for, moving beyond vague desires to a concrete aim.

Assess Your Current Awareness
Emily began reflecting on her existing understanding of her goal:
Excitement: She noted, "Traveling rejuvenates me and inspires my creativity." This acknowledgement of her passion for travel reinforced her determination to make a change.

- Fears: Emily confronted her fears, writing down thoughts like, "What if I lose clients? Will my income drop?" Recognising these fears was crucial in understanding the mental barriers she needed to address.

- Past Experiences: She recalled a previous trip where she successfully delegated tasks to a trusted colleague, which allowed her to enjoy her vacation. This positive experience provided her with a sense of hope and a blueprint for how she could manage her business while traveling in the future.

Through this step, Emily established a strong foundation for her journey, gaining clarity about her goal and the internal challenges she would need to navigate.

Step 2: Resources

Research Options
Emily began brainstorming a variety of resources that could help her achieve her goal of balancing work and travel. She thought broadly and compiled a list:
- Books: She discovered Books which focuses on concepts of delegation and automation in work processes key ideas for reclaiming her time.
- Websites: Emily explored reputable blogs and articles on time management, client relations, and work-life harmony, seeking practical tips that she could implement immediately.
- Podcast: She identified Podcasts, which features stories from successful entrepreneurs who discuss their experiences in managing businesses while enjoying their personal lives.
- Courses: Emily found a course which promised to teach her strategies for assigning tasks efficiently and managing her team more effectively.

- Mentors: She reached out to a fellow entrepreneur in her network who had successfully scaled her business while maintaining a travel lifestyle, seeking advice and insights from her experiences.

Evaluate Resources
- After compiling her list, Emily reviewed each resource to determine which ones would be the most beneficial. She selected three primary resources:
- The book for its strategies on time management and delegation.
- The course to develop her skills in assigning tasks.
- The podcast for ongoing inspiration and practical tips from peers.

Emily took detailed notes on key insights, strategies, and tips from each resource, focusing on those that resonated with her needs and aspirations. This evaluation process helped her narrow down her focus and ensured that she was equipped with relevant knowledge as she moved forward in her journey.

Step 3: Breathe

Breathe for Clarity
Emily set aside time for a quiet meditation session, creating a peaceful environment in her office. She sat comfortably, surrounding herself with her selected resources.

- Closing her eyes, she took several deep breaths, inhaling deeply through her nose, holding for a moment, and exhaling slowly through her mouth.

- As she focused her mind on her goal—creating a work schedule that would allow her to travel—she asked herself, "What would my life look like with this new outlook towards my business and life goals? Which is the best way forward?" She allowed her thoughts to flow freely, without judgement, embracing whatever ideas emerged during this reflective time.

After several minutes of meditation, Emily opened her eyes and began to write down the insights that surfaced. She noted the importance of setting clear boundaries with clients and recognised that she needed to explore outsourcing certain tasks to regain control over her schedule.

Breathe for Visualisation
With her goal and insights in mind, Emily found a comfortable position once again and closed her eyes. This time, she visualised herself successfully achieving her goal: sitting on a sunlit beach, laptop closed, enjoying the sound of waves while knowing her business was thriving back home.

- As she immersed herself in this visualisation, she took deep breaths, experiencing the freedom of choices, feeling happy to enjoy her success and satisfaction of having both a successful business and the freedom to travel. The vivid imagery filled her with motivation and clarity about what she wanted to achieve.

After the visualisation, Emily jotted down the emotions that stood out to her: "Freedom, joy, and satisfaction." This exercise reinforced her commitment to making the necessary changes in her life and provided her with a powerful reminder of why she was pursuing this goal. By connecting deeply with her desired outcome, Emily felt invigorated and ready to take action.

Step 4: Action

Create a Plan
Emily translated her insights into a structured action plan. She broke down her goal into manageable steps:

Short-Term Goals (1 month)
- Identify Tasks for Delegation: Make a list of daily and weekly tasks that can be handed off to others.
- Set Client Boundaries: Clearly communicate her availability to clients, establishing specific times for meetings and responses.

Medium-Term Goals (3-6 months)
- Hire Support for Staff (Virtual Assistant): Begin the process of finding a reliable virtual assistant to manage administrative tasks and support her ongoing projects.
- Revamp Client On-boarding Process: Develop a more structured approach to on-boarding new clients that includes clear expectations and limits on communication.

Long-Term Goals (1 year)
Plan a Travel Trip: Strategise her first trip, ensuring that her business can run smoothly in her absence, potentially visiting a new destination for at least three weeks.

Take Action
Emily started with her first short-term goal by creating a list of tasks that could be delegated, such as social media scheduling, client follow-ups, and basic graphic design. She set a date to communicate her new boundaries to her clients, crafting an email that outlined her availability and the benefits of these changes. To stay organised, she utilised a project management tool to track her tasks and deadlines. She celebrated small wins, such as successfully delegating a week's worth of social media posts and receiving positive feedback from clients about the changes.

Reflect and Adjust
After one month, Emily scheduled a check-in to assess her progress. During this reflection period, she asked herself several key questions:
- What has worked well?: Emily noted that setting boundaries with clients had significantly reduced her stress and allowed her to reclaim time for herself. Clients appreciated her transparency, and many adjusted well to the changes.

- What challenges have I faced? She acknowledged that some clients were initially resistant to her new availability, expressing concern about potential delays in communication.

- Do I need to adjust my plan? Emily realised she needed to provide additional resources to help clients understand the benefits of her new approach. She decided to create a client FAQ document explaining how these changes would enhance her service quality.

With these reflections in mind, Emily adjusted her action plan. She sent out the FAQ to her clients and scheduled one-on-one calls with those who still had concerns. This proactive communication helped alleviate worries and reinforced her commitment to maintaining high service standards.

Emily's journey through the Momentum Matrix has been transformative. By identifying her goal, assessing her current situation, gathering valuable resources, and taking decisive action, she has successfully shifted her work-life harmony. Through clear communication and strategic delegation, she has not only reduced her stress but has also enhanced her client relationships. Emily's proactive approach allowed her to reclaim precious time for herself, paving the way for a more fulfilling lifestyle that integrates both her professional ambitions and her passion for travel.

How Is Emily Doing Now?

Today, Emily is thriving both personally and professionally. With her virtual assistant handling day-to-day administrative tasks, she enjoys a more manageable workload and has the freedom to explore new destinations. She recently completed her first travel trip to Bali, where she spent three weeks enjoying the beach, immersing herself in local culture, and even finding inspiration for her business.

Emily has established a system that allows her to maintain client satisfaction while taking time off. She continues to refine her processes and is now exploring opportunities to expand her business further. Her confidence has grown, and she feels empowered to say no to clients when necessary, ensuring that her work aligns with her values and lifestyle. Overall, Emily's commitment to her goal has not only improved her well-being but has also enhanced her creativity and productivity in her business. She serves as an inspiring example of how structured planning and self-reflection can lead to a balanced life filled with both professional success and personal joy.

Meet Cassy

Cassy is a dedicated mum living in Perth, Australia, with her two lively daughters, a one-year-old and a four-year-old. Alongside her role as a mother, she runs a flourishing floral business that she is passionate about. However, the demands of raising two young children while managing her business have led to feelings of burnout and failing at life. As a perfectionist, Cassy often feels the need to handle every aspect of her business herself, which has compounded her stress and left her struggling to maintain a healthy work-life harmony. Recognising that her business is suffering and that she needs to make a change, Cassy decided to utilise the Momentum Matrix to create a more harmonious and fulfilling lifestyle.

Step 1: Awareness

Identify Your Goal
Cassy took a moment of quiet reflection after her daughters went to bed. She asked herself, "What do I truly want to achieve?" After some contemplation, she articulated her goal: "I want to create a routine that allows me to manage my floral business successfully while being present for my children." This clear vision provided her with direction.

Assess Your Current Awareness
  Cassy began reflecting on her situation by writing down her thoughts:

- Excitement: "I love creating beautiful floral arrangements and bringing joy to my customers."

- Fears: "What if I can't keep up with both my business and my children? Am I letting my family down if I focus on my career?"

Past Experiences: She recalled times when she successfully harmonised work and family during busy seasons, such as weddings, when careful planning allowed her to manage both effectively. This gave her hope that finding both was achievable.

Step 2: Resources

Research Options
Cassy began exploring resources that could help her achieve her goal:
- Books: She discovered a book which focuses on prioritisation and time management.
- Websites: She searched for blogs dedicated to work-life balance for mothers, looking for practical advice and relatable stories.
- Podcasts: A Mum Podcast, featuring discussions on motherhood, entrepreneurship, and self-care.
- Courses: Cassy found an online course for Busy Mums, which promised to equip her with tailored strategies for managing her time effectively.
- Support Groups: She looked into local and online support groups for entrepreneurial mums, aiming to connect with others who face similar challenges.

- Mentors: She reached out to a fellow florist in her network who had successfully scaled her business while maintaining a travel lifestyle, seeking advice and insights from her experiences.

Evaluate Resources

After reviewing her options, Cassy selected three primary resources:
- The book for its insights on focusing on what matters most.
- The online course on time management to gain practical tools for her daily routine.
- The support group for entrepreneurial mums to share experiences and gain encouragement.

She took detailed notes on key strategies and tips from each resource, ensuring she was well-prepared to implement them in her life.

Step 3: Breathe

Breathe for Clarity
Cassy set aside time for a meditation session, creating a calm space in her living room.
- She closed her eyes, took deep breaths, and focused on her goal of achieving work-life harmony.

- During this reflective time, she asked herself, "What steps can I take to create harmony in my life?"

After her meditation, she opened her eyes and wrote down insights that emerged: "I need to establish a daily schedule; chunks of energy that includes being present in work time, family time, and self-care."

Breathe for Visualisation
With her goal in mind, Cassy visualised, feeling a sense of herself successfully managing her business while enjoying quality time with her daughters. She pictured herself working on floral arrangements during their nap times, followed by playful afternoons at the park.

As she visualised, she breathed deeply, immersing herself in the feelings of joy and fulfillment that accompanied this balanced life. After finishing her visualisation, she noted the emotions that stood out: "Peace, joy, and accomplishment."

Step 4: Action

Create a Plan
Cassy developed a structured action plan to achieve her goal:

Short-Term Goals (1 month)
- Establish a Daily Schedule: Create a routine that allocates specific times for work, family activities, and self-care. She planned to dedicate her daughters' nap times for focused work and reserve evenings for family.
- Set Boundaries: Communicate her work hours to family and friends to minimise interruptions during designated work times, ensuring she has uninterrupted focus.

Medium-Term Goals (3-6 months)
- Hire Part-Time Help: Explore the possibility of hiring a part-time assistant to help with floral arrangements during peak seasons.
- Revamp Business Processes: Streamline her business operations to increase efficiency, such as automating order processing and inventory management.

Long-Term Goals (1 year)
- Plan a Family Vacation: Schedule a family trip to create lasting memories, ensuring that her business can run smoothly in her absence through proper delegation and planning.

Take Action
Cassy began by creating her daily schedule, designating specific work hours during her daughters' nap times and after they went to bed. She communicated her availability to her clients, leading to a more manageable workload.
To celebrate her progress, she planned a family outing one weekend, reinforcing the importance of joy and harmony in her life.

Reflect and Adjust
After one month, Cassy scheduled a check-in to review her progress.
She asked herself:
- What has worked well? Cassy found that her new schedule allowed her to be more productive during work hours while being fully present with her children during family time.

- What challenges have I faced? She acknowledged that her perfectionist tendencies sometimes led her to take on too much, making it hard to delegate tasks.

- Do I need to adjust my plan? She decided to implement "quiet time" during her daughters' naps, where she would minimise distractions and focus solely on work.

Cassy adjusted her action plan by setting up a designated workspace away from the main living area to enhance her focus and productivity. This physical boundary helped her signal to her family when she was in work mode. She also reached out to her support group for tips on managing her perfectionism, learning strategies to trust her assistant and let go of the need for everything to be perfect.

Cassy's journey through the Momentum Matrix has been instrumental in helping her achieve a harmonious relationship between her responsibilities as a mother and her passion for her floral business. By clearly defining her goals, gathering valuable resources, and taking actionable steps, she has transformed her daily routine. With her newfound focus and strategies in place, Cassy now enjoys dedicated work time, quality moments with her daughters, and the peace of mind that comes from a well-organised life.

How Is Cassy Doing Today?

Today, Cassy is thriving. She has successfully implemented her daily schedule, allowing her to work productively while being fully present for her children. The part-time help she hired during busy seasons has relieved much of her workload, enabling her to focus on growing her business without feeling overwhelmed.

Cassy has learned to navigate her perfectionist tendencies, recognising when to let go and trust her support system. She recently planned a family getaway, excited to create cherished memories with her daughters. Feeling empowered and rejuvenated, Cassy has cultivated a sense of harmony that seemed elusive just a few months ago. Her story serves as an inspiring reminder of the power of structured planning, self-reflection, and community support in achieving personal and professional fulfillment.

MOMENTUM MATRIX

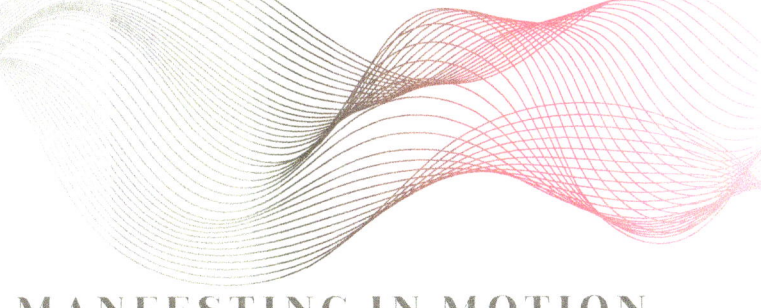

MANFESTING IN MOTION
WORK SHEET

Step 1: Awareness

Identify Your Goal
- Find a quiet space where you can think without interruptions.
- Ask yourself, "What do I truly want to achieve?" Consider both professional and personal aspects.

Write down your goal in a clear and specific manner. For example, instead of " I want to help 50 more clients by...," or "I want to be healthier by...," write "I want to run a 5k in under 30 minutes by the end of the year."

Write Your Statement

Assess Your Current Awareness

Reflect on what you know about your awareness. Write down your thoughts, feelings, and any beliefs related to this goal.

This awareness will serve as a foundation for your journey.

What skills or knowledge do you already possess?

What excites me about this goal?

What fears or doubts do I have?

What past experiences might influence my journey?

Step 2: Resources

Research Options
Start by brainstorming a list of potential resources. Think broadly

Evaluate Resources
- Review your initial list of resources. Choose three that stand out based on your interests and needs.

- If these resources don't provide enough information or inspiration, discard them and search for the next set of three.

Take notes on what you find in each resource.
Highlight key insights, strategies, or tips that resonate with you.

NOTES

Mentors: Consider reaching out to individuals who have achieved similar goals.

Evaluate Resources
Review your initial list of resources. Choose three that stand out based on your interests and needs.

Books: Search for recommended titles in your area of interest.

Website: Look for reputable blogs, online courses, or organisations that specialise in your goal

Podcasts: Identify podcasts that feature experts or success stories related to your goal.

Courses: Explore online platforms for relevant classes.

Step 3: Breathe

Breathe for Clarity

- Set aside time for a quiet meditation session. Sit comfortably with your three resources nearby.
- Close your eyes and take several deep breaths. Inhale deeply through your nose, hold for a moment, and exhale slowly through your mouth.
- Focus your mind on the goal you've identified. Ask yourself, "What is the best way forward?" Allow your thoughts to flow without judgement.
- After a few minutes, open your eyes and write down any insights or ideas that emerged during this time.

This could include new perspectives or steps you hadn't considered.

Breathe for Visualisation

- With your goal and insights in mind, find a comfortable position. Close your eyes again, Visualise or feel yourself successfully achieving your goal.
- Picture or feel the environment, people, and feelings associated with this success. As you do, breathe deeply, immersing yourself in the experience. Feel the joy, excitement, and satisfaction of reaching your goal. (Any positive emotions that come up)
- After visualising, jot down the emotions and images that stood out to you.

This will reinforce your motivation and commitment.

HINT: It's totally normal to struggle with visualisation. If that happens, just go with your gut instinct! Tune into how you're feeling and notice where that sensation sits in your body.

Step 4: Action

Create a Plan
Take your insights and break them down into actionable steps. Use the following structure as a guide: (feel free to adjust it to fit your timeline; it can span 2 to 3 months before or after your term goals).

Consider the following structure:

- Short-Term Goals: Identify what you can achieve in the next week or month.

- Medium-Term Goals: Outline what you wish to accomplish in the next three to six months.

- Long-Term Goal: Define your ultimate goal and set a timeline for achieving it.

Write your plan in a format that works for you, such as a table, bullet points, or a mind map.

Take Action

- Start with the first task on your list. Set a specific date and time to work on it.

- Use tools like calendars, to-do lists, or project management apps to stay organised and track your progress.

- Celebrate small wins along the way to keep your motivation high.

Short-Term Goals

Identify what you can achieve in the next week or month.

Medium-Term Goals

Outline what you wish to accomplish in the next three to six months.

Long-Term Goal

Define your ultimate goal and set a timeline for achieving it.

Reflect and Adjust

Schedule regular check-ins (weekly or monthly) to review your progress.

Ask yourself:
- What has worked well so far?

- What challenges have I faced?

- Do I need to adjust my plan or seek new resources?

Make necessary adjustments to your action plan based on your reflections.
Stay flexible and open to change as you progress toward your goal. (It doesn't need to be perfect)

By following these detailed steps in the Momentum Matrix, you can effectively transform your awareness into actionable steps.
This structured approach will empower you to build confidence, leverage resources, and take decisive actions toward achieving your professional and personal goals.

MOMENTUM MATRIX

Reflect and Adjust

What has worked well so far?

What challenges have I faced?

Do I need to adjust my plan or seek new resources?

Gratitude is the Force that Lifts You

"Success is liking yourself,
liking what you do,
and liking how you do it."
- Maya Angelou

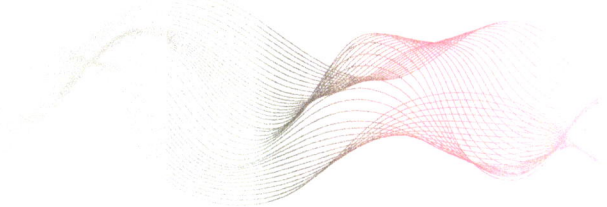

Gratitude

Pathway to Confidence and Success

Let's talk about gratitude and why it's such a game changer for women in both their professional and personal lives. Practicing gratitude can be a powerful force that propels you forward, creating momentum toward your success. It's like having a secret weapon in your arsenal, think of it as your magical cape that helps you fly over obstacles!

When you take the time to reflect on what you're grateful for, it shifts your focus from what's missing to what's already in your life.

By acknowledging the support, achievements, and experiences that have shaped your journey, you create a sense of empowerment that fuels your motivation. It's like giving yourself a little pep talk that says, "Hey, you've got this, now go conquer the world!"

Research shows that gratitude can significantly boost your mental well-being and resilience (Emmons & McCullough, 2003). When you cultivate a grateful mindset, you're more likely to tackle challenges with a positive attitude. Instead of feeling overwhelmed by obstacles, you see them as opportunities for growth. This is crucial for women striving to break barriers and achieve their goals. Gratitude turns those "uh-oh" moments into "aha!" moments—and who doesn't love a good lightbulb moment?

Plus, practicing gratitude reinforces your sense of purpose. When you recognise the people and experiences that have contributed to your success, it connects your goals to something larger than yourself. This connection can be incredibly motivating, especially when the going gets tough. Instead of questioning your path, you remind yourself of the impact you want to make and the support you have along the way. It's a powerful reminder that you're not in this alone—unless you're trying to assemble IKEA furniture, in which case, good luck!

Incorporating gratitude into your daily routine can also help you keep that momentum going. Whether it's jotting down a few things you appreciate in a journal or sharing your gratitude with a colleague, these small practices create a ripple effect of positivity. When you focus on the good, it energizes you to take action toward your goals. It's like lighting a fire under you that pushes you to tackle that project or go for that promotion—without actually burning your pants off!

And let's not forget how expressing gratitude can strengthen your professional relationships. When you acknowledge the contributions of others, it fosters a supportive environment where collaboration flourishes. This is particularly beneficial for women, as building a strong network can open doors to new opportunities and mentorship. When you lift others up, you create a community that encourages everyone to grow and succeed, like a sisterhood of superwomen!

Now, let's dig into how gratitude can elevate your vibration to joy. When you consciously practice gratitude, you start to shift your emotional state. This shift raises your vibrational frequency, making you feel lighter and more connected to positive energy.

According to Dr. David Hawkins, in his book "Power vs. Force", higher vibrations correlate with positive emotions like love, joy, and gratitude, while lower vibrations are linked to negative emotions. So, when you choose gratitude, you're literally tuning yourself to a higher frequency.

This elevated state of joy doesn't just benefit you; it ripples out to everyone around you. Think of it as your own little joy generator. When you're vibrating at a higher frequency, that energy becomes contagious! People are naturally drawn to positivity, and your gratitude can inspire those around you to adopt a similar mindset. Research has shown that positive emotions can spread within social networks, creating a ripple effect of increased well-being. (Fowler & Christakis, 2008).

Moreover, this joyful energy can influence every area of your life. Whether it's in your relationships, work, or personal pursuits, when you radiate gratitude and joy, you attract more of what you want. You begin to notice opportunities and connections that you might have overlooked before. It's like putting on a pair of joy-colored glasses, you suddenly see the world in a whole new light! Studies have found that individuals who practice gratitude experience improved relationships, enhanced work performance, and greater overall life satisfaction (Wood, Froh, & Geraghty, 2010).

Additionally, gratitude can bolster your resilience during tough times. When you cultivate a habit of looking for things to be thankful for, you build a mental toolkit that helps you navigate challenges with grace. This resilience is crucial, especially for women who often face unique pressures in both their personal and professional lives. Rather than feeling defeated by setbacks, gratitude encourages you to bounce back and keep moving forward, armed with the knowledge that there's always something good to hold onto.

In the end, gratitude isn't just a nice sentiment; it's a strategic approach that can enhance your professional and personal life. By embracing gratitude, you'll find yourself more motivated, resilient, and connected to your purpose. So, are you ready to practice gratitude and watch it transform your journey? Let's get started, your future self will thank you!

Seven Days of Gratitude

Raising you higher.

For the upcoming seven days, take a moment to reflect and jot down at least three things, people, or experiences—whether big or small—that you are grateful for.

DAY ONE

DAY TWO

Seven Days of Gratitude

Raising you higher.

DAY THREE

DAY FOUR

DAY FIVE

Seven Days of Gratitude

Raising you higher.

DAY SIX

DAY SEVEN

How quickly did your energy transform once you embraced gratitude in your daily life?
Just imagine the profound shift in your mindset over a lifetime and the joy that this practice can bring.

You Are The Inspiration

Dear Beautiful Soul,

As you embark on your healing journey, remember that your steps are not taken in isolation. Every moment of grace and gratitude you embrace radiates outward, touching the lives of those around you. Your courage to heal not only transforms your own life but becomes a beacon for others, showing them the way towards their own light. You have the power to inspire without even realising it, simply by being true to yourself.

We, as women, share an innate connection that transcends words. When you honour your own journey and choose compassion over self-criticism, you create a ripple effect that fosters understanding and empathy among us all. By nurturing yourself, you give others permission to do the same, cultivating a community of support and love. Together, we can lift each other up and celebrate our unique paths.

In moments of struggle, remind yourself that you are not alone. Each challenge you face is an opportunity to grow and deepen your connection to yourself and others. By showing up authentically, you invite those around you to embrace their own vulnerabilities and strengths. Your journey is a testament to the resilience and beauty that resides within you, and it encourages others to find the courage to heal as well.

As you walk this path, may you always remember the incredible impact you have. Your grace is a gift to the world, and your gratitude enriches every soul you encounter. Together, let us continue to support and uplift one another, creating a world where love and understanding flourish. Thank you for being the remarkable woman you are.

Tori xoxo

REFERENCES

Goleman, D. (1988). "Working with Emotional Intelligence" New York: Bantam Books.
Goleman, D. (1995). "Emotional Intelligence: Why It Can Matter More Than IQ." New York: Bantam Books.
Neff, K. D. (2003). "Self-compassion: An alternative conceptualization of a healthy attitude toward oneself." "Self and Identity, 2" (2), 85-101.
Doidge, N. (2007). "The Brain That Changes Itself: Stories of Personal Triumph from the Frontiers of Brain Science." New York: Viking.
Kabat-Zinn, J. (2003). "Mindfulness-Based Interventions in Context: Past, Present, and Future." "Clinical Psychology: Science and Practice, 10" (2), 144-156.
Mohr, T. (2014). "Playing Big: Practical Wisdom for Women Who Want to Speak Up, Create, and Lead." New York: Perigee.
Kay, K., & Shipman, J. (2014). "The Confidence Code: The Science and Art of Self-Assurance—What Women Should Know." New York: HarperBusiness.
Goyal, M., Singh, S., Sibinga, E. M. S., & et al. (2014). "Meditation Programs for Psychological Stress and Well-being: A Systematic Review and Meta-analysis." JAMA Internal Medicine.
Keng, S. L., Smoski, M. J., & Robins, C. J. (2011). "Effects of mindfulness on psychological health: A review of empirical studies. Clinical Psychology Review."
Fredrickson, B. L. (2001). "The Role of Positive Emotions in Positive Psychology: The Broaden-and-Build Theory of Positive Emotions." American Psychologist.
Bravery, J. (2020). "Journal of Personality and Social Psychology."
"Out-of-the-box." K. (2021). Creativity Research Journal.
Networking, L. (2022). Harvard Business Review.
Neuroscience for You, (2023). Journal of Neuropsychology.

REFERENCES

Dietrich, A. (2004). "The cognitive neuroscience of creativity." Psychological Bulletin, 130(6), 822-853.

Hughes, K., & O'Brien, C. (2020). "The Role of Creativity in Enhancing Well-Being." Journal of Positive Psychology, 15(2), 175-184.

Kaimal, G., Ray, K., & Muniz, R. (2016). "Art-making and well-being: A review of the evidence." Journal of the American Art Therapy Association, 33(2), 201-207.

Pennebaker, J. W., & Chung, C. K. (2011). "Expressive writing: Connections to physical and mental health." The Oxford Handbook of Health Psychology, 417-437.

Locke, E. A., & Latham, G. P. (2002). "Building a Practically Useful Theory of Goal Setting and Task Motivation: A 35-Year Odyssey." American Psychologist.

Duhigg, C. (2012). "The Power of Habit: Why We Do What We Do in Life and Business." Random House.

Emmons, R. A., & McCullough, M. E. (2003). "Counting Blessings Versus Burdens: An Experimental Investigation of Gratitude and Subjective Well-Being in Daily Life." Journal of Personality and Social Psychology.

Hawkins, D. R. (1995). "Power vs. Force: The Hidden Determinants of Human Behavior." Hay House.

Fowler, J. H., & Christakis, N. A. (2008). "Dynamic Spread of Happiness in a Large Social Network: Longitudinal Analysis Over 20 Years in the Framingham Heart Study." BMJ.

Wood, A. M., Froh, J. J., & Geraghty, A. W. (2010). "Gratitude and Well-Being: A Review and Theoretical Integration." Clinical Psychology Review.

ACKNOWLEDGEMENT
With Gratitude

As I reflect on the journey of writing this book, I am filled with profound gratitude for the incredible support system that has surrounded me. To my family, thank you for being my unwavering foundation. Your love, encouragement, and belief in my dreams have made all the difference in my life. I am truly blessed to have you by my side through every step of this journey.

I would also like to extend my heartfelt thanks to the remarkable women in my life who have shared their challenges and triumphs with me. Your stories have inspired and empowered me, teaching me invaluable lessons about resilience and the true essence of courage. Your willingness to be vulnerable has given me clarity on what truly matters, helping me to navigate my own path with confidence and purpose.

This book serves as a reflection of the valuable lessons I have learned from those around me, lessons that have shaped my success both professionally and personally. It is my hope to give back by sharing these insights, which have been instrumental in my growth. Through these pages, I aim to inspire others to embrace their journeys, learn from their challenges, and recognise the strength that lies within. By passing on what I've learned, I wish to empower others to achieve their own dreams and navigate life with confidence and purpose.

Thank you all for being my pillars of strength and for guiding me as I navigate this journey called life. I am thrilled to share this work with you and to witness more incredible women harmonising their lives while achieving their dreams.

With all my love and appreciation

Tori xoxo

ABOUT THE AUTHOR

Tori G. Doyle, a seasoned mindset coach for women based in Sunny Queensland, Australia. With over three decades of shared experiences with her husband, Tori finds solace in life's simple pleasures and the serenity of her surroundings, infusing her coaching practice with a profound sense of gratitude and harmony.

Having triumphed over her own struggles with negative internal dialogue, Tori is passionate about sharing the liberating concept of "good enough" with her clients. As a certified NLP coach and transpersonal therapist, she brings a wealth of knowledge and compassion to her work, guiding women through life's complexities with grace and resilience.

Her approach is characterised by a blend of positivity, laughter, and tailored support, creating transformative experiences that uplift and inspire. Tori is a firm believer in the innate strength and potential of every woman, striving to empower her clients to embrace joy, cultivate resilience, and find harmony in their daily lives. With heartfelt dedication, she provides a safe and nurturing space for women to explore their true selves and embark on a journey of growth and fulfillment.

Join Tori on a transformative path towards happiness, harmony, and professional and personal empowerment. Together, let's unlock the endless possibilities that lie within each woman, as we embark on a journey of self-discovery, laughter, and fulfillment.

The Path To Confidence Project

There's more to come

Get ready to embark on a transformative journey with my upcoming series, born from a passion I proudly call the Path to Confidence Project. Each book reflects the challenges I faced on my path to self-discovery, empowerment, and growth. From battling self-doubt and imposter syndrome to navigating the complexities of work-life ~~balance~~ harmony, I've experienced firsthand the struggles that many women face. These books are designed to resonate with anyone who has ever felt overwhelmed, lost, or unrecognised in their journey.

Within these pages, I'll share the proven strategies and practical tools that helped me reclaim my confidence and find my unique rhythm in life. Each volume dives deep into the obstacles we encounter, offering relatable stories and actionable insights that empower you to overcome your own hurdles. Whether you're grappling with perfectionism, societal pressures, or the fear of rejection, you'll discover that you're not alone, and there's a way forward.

This is more than just a collection of books; it's a heartfelt invitation to embrace your authentic self and step into your power. I'm excited to share what I've learned and support you in your own journey toward confidence and fulfillment.

Together, let's break down barriers and cultivate a life where you can thrive unapologetically.

Stay tuned for the launch of these empowering books!

CONNECT

Certified Mindset Coach and Transpersonal Therapist for Women Who Do It All

Empowering women to embrace their multifaceted lives, Tori specialises in helping women navigate the challenges of juggling careers, business, family, and personal aspirations.
With a warm and encouraging approach, she guides her clients toward a mindset that fosters resilience, harmony, happiness and fulfillment.

What Tori Offers:

- Coaching Sessions: Personalised one-on-one coaching tailored to your unique journey. Tori provides the tools and strategies you need to break through barriers and achieve your life goals.

- Workshops: Engaging and interactive workshops designed to inspire and equip women with practical skills for personal and professional growth. Join a community of like-minded women and discover new ways to thrive.

- Retreats: Transformative retreats that offer a chance to step back, REVIVE, and reconnect with yourself. Immerse yourself in a nurturing environment, away from the daily grind, and focus on your personal development.

Connect with Tori:
For more information on coaching, workshops, and retreats, or to book a session, visit her website: www.toridoyle.au

Flames to Freedom

MEDITATION

FLAMES TO FREEDOM

Guided Meditation

Start with a few slow, deep breaths through your nose, slowing your breath even more as you exhale. In and out, and as you do, your whole body will become relaxed. Breathe in and relax your feet, let them fall naturally. Relax your calves, thighs, hips, allowing your body to sink into the floor. Relax all your stomach muscles, your chest, shoulders, arms, and hands. Let your fingers drop. Relax your neck muscles, your jaw, eyes, and brow. Your whole body is completely relaxed, supported, and safe.

In this state of relaxation, prepare to release the negative self-talk that has weighed you down. Visualise a time when these thoughts were most present, when they felt overwhelming. Acknowledge them without judgment, simply recognising their presence in your life.

Imagine these negative thoughts written on a piece of paper. See the words clearly, and feel any emotions associated with them. It's normal to feel their weight, but know this is the moment of release. Visualise a warm, inviting flame before you, perhaps a candle or campfire, flickering gently.

Bring the paper with the negative statements closer to the flame. As you do, feel the tension and heaviness associated with these thoughts begin to lift. The flame dances with anticipation, ready to transform these words into nothingness.

MEDITATION

FLAMES TO FREEDOM

Guided Meditation *cont.*

Now, watch as the paper ignites. The flames consume it, turning it to ash. As the smoke rises, visualise the negative self-talk dissipating into the air, leaving you lighter and freer. Feel a sense of relief and release wash over you.

With the negativity released, focus on the space within you that is now open and ready to be filled with positivity. Visualise a glowing light in your mind, the embodiment of your positive affirmation. This is your new belief, strong and radiant.

Allow this positive affirmation to grow brighter, filling every part of your being. Feel its warmth and strength infuse your body with love and compassion. You are worthy, capable, and deserving of all good things.

As you embrace this new belief, imagine it settling into your heart, becoming an integral part of who you are. Feel the energy of this affirmation expanding within you, creating a foundation of positivity and self-love.

Take a deep breath in, and as you exhale, feel this energy connect with the universal source. Let it flow through you, expanding outward into the world, bringing support, love, and safety to everyone around you.

MEDITATION

FLAMES TO FREEDOM

Guided Meditation *Cont.*

Take a moment to let these feelings settle, honoring your journey of self-exploration and transformation. Allow the warmth of this new energy to embrace you fully, knowing you have the power to create positive change in your life.

You are beautiful and of divine worth, supported by the universe. You are loved unconditionally and held in the embrace of infinite possibilities.
Let this truth guide you always.

When you are ready, gently move your body, roll your hands and feet, allowing yourself to come back to the present moment. Slowly sit up, carrying with you the sense of empowerment and worthiness you have cultivated.

Thank you for taking this journey of release and renewal. Embrace the freedom and strength you have discovered, and let it guide you forward.

NOTES

THE ULTIMATE BURN BOOK FOR THE SUCCESSFUL WOMAN WITHIN

NOTES